TEMPO

GOLF'S MASTER KEY: HOW TO FIND IT, HOW TO KEEP IT

TEMPO

GOLF'S MASTER KEY: HOW TO FIND IT, HOW TO KEEP IT

by AL GEIBERGER

with Larry Dennis

A Golf Digest Book

PHOTO CREDITS

All photos by John Newcomb, Tony Rose and Steve Szurlej
except page 12, Wide World Photos; page 15, Richard Pilling;
page 16, Mel Page; and page 22, United Press International.

Published by Golf Digest/Tennis, Inc.
A New York Times Company
5520 Park Avenue
Box 395
Trumbull, Connecticut 06611-0395

Trade book distribution by
Simon and Schuster
A Division of Simon & Schuster, Inc.
Simon & Schuster Building
Rockefeller Center
1230 Avenue of the Americas
New York, New York 10020

Third Printing
First Paperback Printing
ISBN 0-914178-82-2
Library of Congress 79-52550
Manufactured in the
United States of America
Printing and binding by
Halliday Lithograph

TABLE OF CONTENTS

ABOUT AL GEIBERGER

If there is a player in professional golf more qualified to write about tempo than Al Geiberger, I'm afraid he is unknown to me. Geiberger is without equal on the subject, for several reasons.

To begin with, his own swing tempo is ideal, as judged by those toughest of critics, his peers. Says Tom Watson, "Al's tempo is the model from which everybody should try to learn. His swing has very much the pendulum type of motion that should be achieved."

Hale Irwin, a two-time U.S. Open champion and himself owner of one of the game's smoothest swings, says, "Allen has probably one of the least-forced swings that I've seen. Most of us tend to speed up under pressure, but Allen maintains a nice, even pace whether he's in the lead or not. It's the biggest single reason he's had such great success."

But most players play and most teachers teach, and seldom do the twain meet. Geiberger is the exception. He is a keen student of the swing, his own and others. He can talk about it thoughtfully and articulately, and he can relate to amateurs at any level. He teaches countless players at the dozen or more clinics he gives around the country each year, and one of his off-tour hobbies is teaching his own three sons.

"Most of my theories have evolved from trying to find a quick way to help players at the clinics I give," Al says. "And I've learned an awful lot about the swing in working with my own boys."

His approach to the swing and its tempo is refreshingly simple. There are indeed mental keys that help achieve good tempo or pace in a golf swing, and they are explored thoroughly in this book. But Geiberger's temple of tempo is built not on gimmicks but on a foundation of solid fundamentals. Tall for a golfer at 6–2 and 170 pounds, he practices what he preaches and teaches.

"Al has the best-looking swing for a tall man I've ever seen," says Bob Toski, who knows a little about such things. "He is fundamentally very sound. He has such good body control, he shifts his weight nice and smoothly and he's a beautiful arm swinger. He has a swing all golfers should try to emulate, because they can be consistent with it."

Geiberger, for certain, has been consistent with it. In a way, it is almost a shame that Al shot that incredible 59 in 1977, because that one flash of brilliance might obscure the fact that he has been a remarkable player for more than 20 years. In a career checkered by illness, injury and personal problems, he has won a dozen tournaments on the PGA Tour, including the 1966 PGA Championship and the 1975 Tournament Players Championship. At the start of the 1981 season he was 16th on the list of all-time money-winners with $1,184,454 in career earnings.

Now 43, Geiberger began winning in 1954 at the age of 16, capturing the National Jaycee Junior and the French International Junior in Paris. He was graduated from the University of Southern California with a degree in business in 1959 and capped a successful amateur career by winning 11 consecutive tournaments. He joined the tour in 1960, finished 37th on the money list that first year and increased his earnings every year for the next eight seasons. He won his first tournament, the Ontario Open, in 1962 and walked off with the PGA Championship at Firestone C.C. in 1966.

He was not to win again until 1974, although his real slump did not begin until 1969. Then, troubled by an inflamed colon and marital difficulties, he dropped out of the top 60 the next four years. It was during this period that the smooth tempo of his swing came to the rescue, at least psychologically.

"I would get comments from fellow players or from people in the gallery on what a nice swing I had and how wonderfully I hit the ball," Al says. "When you are doubting yourself, that's the kind of encouragement you need to keep fighting on and keep playing instead of throwing in the towel. Actually, during most of my slump I did hit the ball fairly well. Most of my problems were either mental or with my putting. If I hadn't had such a solid game from tee to green, I might not have made it through that down period."

Geiberger's second marriage, to the former Lynn Butler, in 1973 signalled the start of his comeback. "Because of my intestinal problems, it had been suggested that I cut back on my playing schedule," he says. "But by playing in a limited number of tournaments, I couldn't perform as well. The fewer chances you have, the more pressure there is to produce. Lynn didn't know much about golf, but she talked to the other players, who told her that I should play more. She finally convinced me, and when I started playing more I started playing better."

Back in the top 60 with more than $63,000 in 1973, he finally broke through to win again at the Sahara Invitational late in 1974.

"That really meant a lot to me," he says. "Because I had gone so long without winning and was beginning to doubt whether I would ever win again, it was a big moment in my life and a real turnaround for me."

The victory gave him his best money-winning year ever at $91,628, but it was only a prelude. In 1975, Al won the Tournament of Champions and the Tournament Players Championship and finished sixth on the money list with $175,693. In 1976, he won the Greater Greensboro Open and the Western Open, tied for second in the U.S. Open and was the No. 5 money-winner with $194,821.

Then, in the summer of the next season, came the victory at the Danny Thomas-Memphis Classic that was highlighted by his second-round 59, the only time 60 ever has been broken on the PGA Tour.

"The highlight of my career probably is winning the PGA Championship," Al says, "but I have a hunch I'll be identified with that 59 for a long time, unless somebody comes along and breaks it. A lot of players have won the PGA, but fortunately I've been the only player to shoot 59."

In January, 1978, Geiberger underwent surgery for removal of a benign growth in his colon and never regained his form, slumping to earnings of just $20,477. But in May of 1979 he snapped out of a putting slump to win his 12th tournament, the Colonial National Invitation. Later that year, however, he was back in the hospital for knee surgery to remove a loose piece of cartilage. No sooner had he recovered from that than he began to suffer increasingly severe abdominal pain. After discovering a noncancerous condition that caused large polyps to develop and block the colon, the surgeons removed Geiberger's colon and performed an ileostomy in September of 1980. Now on the mend from that, Al is looking forward to another "comeback."

"It seems I like to make these little comebacks now and then," he smiles. "Actually, that's what the tour is about. It's very hard to be a consistent winner, or even to be a consistent player all the time. I think the consistency of my play is my strongest point, but when you play for as many years as I have you are bound to have your ups and downs. The key to success on the tour—or at any level of play, for that matter—is not letting the down period get to you and make your game worse than it is. You just have to be patient and work your way out of it.

"Golf is a sport of self-discipline. It's an individual sport. You are completely responsible when you play badly, which is why it is so depressing. You can't blame anyone else, and there is no one else on the team who can help you. On the other hand, when you play well and win, it is so rewarding because you know you did it yourself. The team didn't carry you through."

I did not get to know Al Geiberger well until we began to collaborate on this book. The loss is mine, for a couple of very good reasons. In the first place, Al is one of the truly nice men I have met, in golf or anywhere else, and to know a nice person is an enviable privilege. Secondly, as a golfer of some avidness—or rabidness—I had waited far too many years to find someone who could help me with a swing tempo which, at best, could be characterized as erratic. Now I have found that someone.

I think you will too.

Larry Dennis
Norwalk, Conn.
January, 1981

OFFICIAL SCORECARD
Danny Thomas Memphis Classic
1977

	7	8	9	Out		10	11	12	13	14	15	16	17	18	In	Total
	564	479	403	3634		417	376	218	464	447	200	512	433	548	3615	7249
				36											36	72
	4	4	3			3	4	2	4	4	2	4	3	4		
				29											30	59

JUN 10 1977
June,

On completion of the round, this card shall be signed by the scorer, verified
and signed by the contestant and handed to scorer's table.

Contestant's Signature

"59! 59! 59!"

It was Friday, June 10, 1977, and it was hot in Memphis. The second round of the Danny Thomas Memphis Classic was being played that day at Colonial Country Club, a 7,249-yard, par-72 course that is one of the toughest we play on the PGA Tour. It also was not in very good shape, the Bermuda greens stubbly and the fairways thinned out so badly by a winter freeze that we were playing preferred lies.

So I really didn't wake up that morning thinking I was going to shoot 59. To be honest, I was thinking about trying to make the 36-hole cut. I had missed the cut in my last two tournaments, and I had spent the week before at home feeling pretty discouraged about my game. On Thursday at Memphis I shot 72 and it looked like 144 would be the cut, which it was. That meant I would need another 72 to stick around the last two days of the tournament. As it turned out, I didn't have to worry.

I really did have reason to be a little confident. About a month before the Memphis tournament I had made a small swing change. Actually, it was a change in my setup position that resulted in a swing change. I had been working with my son Rob at home, trying to get him to lower his hands a little bit at address, when suddenly I realized my hands had got too high, too. So I straightened my legs a little and bent over more from my hips. This dropped my hands a bit and gave me the feeling of staying down and through the ball longer during my swing. With my hands high, I felt as if they were turning over too quickly at impact. When I lowered them, the hands and clubhead moved together through the impact area for a longer period of time. When I hit three-quarter wedge shots, I could make a nice body turn and my hands would finish straight out in front of me. So I carried that feeling over into the full swing, and it worked. I felt I had been hitting the ball well in previous weeks, but I had been putting so poorly that it didn't show on the scoreboard.

I had blown a three-foot putt on the last green to miss the cut at Atlanta by a stroke. I was choking to death because my stroke was so bad. If you are fundamentally sound, you are able to perform even under severe pressure. But my putting was at the bottom of the barrel at the moment. So I went to the putting green for some practice after the round. My caddie, Lee Lynch, told me my stance was closed, my feet aiming to the right of the target, and I was taking the putter back inside my target line on the backswing. This was causing me to loop the putter around to get it back on line, which in turn killed my acceleration. I couldn't stroke through the putt, couldn't keep a good movement going toward the hole because I was too busy trying to get the putterface square to my target.

During the next week at home I didn't feel like playing or even practicing. But while working in my office, I would occasionally get up and putt a little on the rug. I opened my stance and stroked putts, and I began to realize that this was making sense. It felt almost as if I were cutting or slicing the putts, but this was because I had gone so far to the opposite extreme. In reality, my stance and stroke probably were pretty square.

During Wednesday's pro-am at Memphis my putting was better, and in the first round Thursday I had rolled the ball pretty well. I had not made a lot of putts—maybe because the greens were rough—but I was feeling more and more confident about my putting. I knew I was on the right track. How right I was I had no way of foreseeing.

Friday I started on the 10th hole, a 417-yard par 4. (The field alternates starting on the first and tenth tees on the first two days of each regular PGA tournament.) I hit a big drive and a 179-yard 6-iron 45 feet past the hole. Normally I would hit a 4- or 5-iron on that hole, so this tipped me off that I was a little pumped up. It was a pattern that was to continue for the rest of the round. I was hitting the ball very solidly and farther than normal, and the farther along in the round I got, the better I hit it.

On the 10th hole I made that 45-footer for birdie. On the 11th, a 376-yarder, I hit a 2-iron and an 8-iron to within 15 feet and stroked a good putt that went right over the edge and just missed. On the 12th, a tough 218-yard par 3, I hit a 4-iron 14 feet away and knocked the putt right in the middle of the hole. As Dave Stockton, one of my playing partners, said later, if the cup had been the size of a cocktail glass, I would have made all my putts, because every one of them was dead in the center.

On the 13th, a 464-yard par 4, I hit another long drive and a 7-iron 30 feet past the hole. It is a tough, sloping green, and I ran my first putt about five feet past the cup. But I drilled it right in the middle coming back. That was a crucial putt, one that often gets overlooked in talk about my round.

The 447-yard 14th was the only hole on which I conceivably could have improved my round. I hit a drive and a 7-iron 161 yards to within eight feet, and as I stood over the putt I heard a fire truck go by. I backed off and looked up and saw a big cloud of smoke close by. After the fire truck went past, I addressed the ball again and hit a good putt, but the

grain got me and the putt didn't break the way I had anticipated.

I was kicking myself for having missed that one, but then the peanut butter crackers arrived. Bob Schreiber, who lives close to the 14th green, had made them up and brought them to me because of my reputation for eating peanut butter sandwiches on the course for quick energy. Not surprisingly, one of my nicknames on tour is Skippy.

I ate four or five of the crackers on the spot, and I'm sure Bob thinks he's responsible for the 59, because I played the next seven holes in eight under par. At any rate, he has brought me peanut butter crackers during every round I have played at Memphis since.

On the 15th hole, a 200-yard par 3, I hit a 3-iron and made a 15-footer for birdie. The 16th is a 512-yard par 5, and I knocked my second shot over the green with a 4-wood. I chipped back to within five feet and made it for birdie.

I had started at 12:32 p.m., in the heat of the day. By now the temperature was close to 100 degrees and the humidity was high. In

Playing partner Jerry McGee

retrospect, that was fortunate for me. I become very uncomfortable in hot weather, but my tempo also seems to be the best at those times. That's probably because I am thinking more of surviving the round without collapsing. The heat also makes me feel tired, which slows me down even more.

On this particular day the adrenaline really began to flow, and I began to swing harder and harder. That usually happens under pressure, and often I have to make a conscious effort to swing easier in such situations. But this time I was ready for it because of the heat. My swing stayed in the groove, my tempo remained good, and as the round went by I hit the ball better and better. As a result, I was hitting it 15 or 20 yards farther without forcing it.

The 17th hole provides a good example of how far I was hitting it that day. It's a 433-yarder on which I usually need a 3- to 5-iron to reach the green. On this day I hit it with an 8-iron from 151 yards away and made a 12-foot putt for the birdie.

At this point my only thought was, "Well, this is a good round, let's keep it going." On the 18th, a 548-yard par 5, I laid up with a 5-iron on my second shot because of a big lake in front of the green, then pitched to within 12 feet and made it. I thought, "Well, wow, that's 30!" I couldn't remember the last time I had shot 30.

The first hole of the golf course, my 10th of the day, is a 582-yard par 5. I hit such a big drive that I was able to go for the green on my second shot. That's something I don't normally do, because there is a trap about 50 yards from the green that you must clear. Most players lay up short of it, because a bunker shot from that far out is one of the toughest you can have, and you don't want it on a potential birdie hole. This time I cleared the bunker and ended up green-high but down a slope to the right. I had about a 30-yard wedge shot, and I holed it for an eagle!

Now I was six under par for the last five holes, and that's when I told myself to go for the record of eight consecutive holes under par. Bob Goalby and Fuzzy Zoeller both had made eight straight birdies, and the odds against that many in a row are pretty incredible.

On the second hole, a 414-yarder, I hit a drive and a pitching wedge 18 feet short of the cup. When I stepped up to the putt, I was not as worried about it as I might have been at other times. I just thought I'd give it my best, and I rolled it right in the middle of the hole. Everything was rolling off the putter so perfectly.

At this point I had it seven under for six holes, nine under for the day. The next hole is a par 3 of 182 yards on the scorecard, although it might not have been playing quite that long that day because the pin was in the front of the green. I knocked a 7-iron 20 feet past the hole, which even now is hard for me to believe. I had a putt that broke about a foot and a half, and it just turned over at the end and went right in the middle. Didn't even flirt with the edge—just went in dead-center.

All I could do was look up at Dave and Jerry McGee, my other playing partner, and think, "Sorry, guys, what am I going to do?" Poor Dave, a two-time PGA champion and million-dollar winner who is one of the best putters ever on tour, couldn't get it in from two feet that day. He was missing everything and shot 75. As Dave tells it, here is this record round being shot, the whole world is watching and he's having one of his worst days. He is constantly being asked to tell the story, and somebody invariably asks him what he shot that day. He always wishes it could have been at least 69 or something respectable instead of 75.

Now I was eight under for seven holes, and my gallery was getting bigger and bigger. The next hole would determine if I tied Goalby and Zoeller. It was a 423-yard par 4 to which I normally hit a 5-, 6- or 7-iron on my second shot. On this day I was hooking the ball a little bit, which is not my style. I got it around the corner of the dogleg, had only 122 yards left, and hit a pitching wedge to the green, about 13 feet from the cup. The hole was on a plateau and I didn't quite get up on it. I hit a good putt,

OFFICIAL

Danny Thoma

Contestant ___Al Geiberger___

Holes	1	2	3	4	5	6	7	8	9	Out
Yards	582	414	182	423	199	388	564	479	403	3634
Par	5	4	3	4	3	4	5	4	4	36
Score	3	3	2	4	3	3	4	4	3	29

Scores must be verified and recorded at each hole.
Questions in dispute must be referred to the Rules Committee.

Marker's Signature ___Dave Stockton___

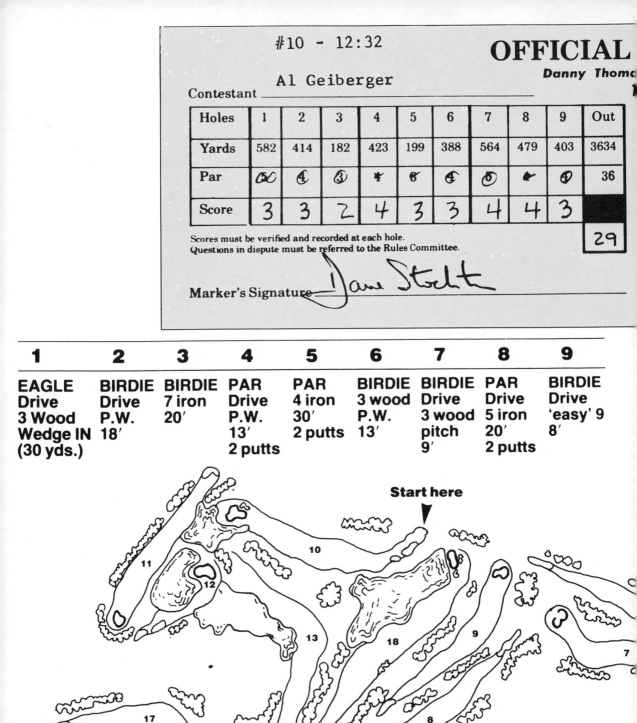

1	2	3	4	5	6	7	8	9
EAGLE	**BIRDIE**	**BIRDIE**	**PAR**	**PAR**	**BIRDIE**	**BIRDIE**	**PAR**	**BIRDIE**
Drive	Drive	7 iron	Drive	4 iron	3 wood	Drive	Drive	Drive
3 Wood	P.W.	20'	P.W.	30'	P.W.	3 wood	5 iron	'easy' 9
Wedge IN	18'		13'	2 putts	13'	pitch	20'	8'
(30 yds.)			2 putts			9'	2 putts	

Start here

10

11

12

13

18

9

7

17

8

14

16

15

**Colonial Country Club
Memphis, Tennessee**

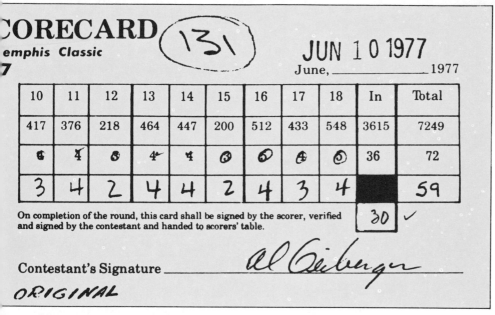

CORECARD

emphis Classic

7

(131)

JUN 1 0 1977

June, _____ 1977

10	11	12	13	14	15	16	17	18	In	Total
417	376	218	464	447	200	512	433	548	3615	7249
6	4	6	4	4	3	5	4	5	36	72
3	4	2	4	4	2	4	3	4		59
							30	✓		

On completion of the round, this card shall be signed by the scorer, verified and signed by the contestant and handed to scorers' table.

Contestant's Signature _____ *Al Geiberger* _____

ORIGINAL

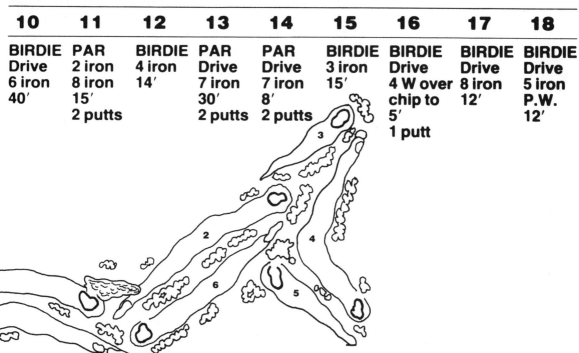

10	**11**	**12**	**13**	**14**	**15**	**16**	**17**	**18**
BIRDIE	PAR	BIRDIE	PAR	PAR	BIRDIE	BIRDIE	BIRDIE	BIRDIE
Drive	2 iron	4 iron	Drive	Drive	3 iron	Drive	Drive	Drive
6 iron	8 iron	14'	7 iron	7 iron	15'	4 W over	8 iron	5 iron
40'	15'		30'	8'		chip to	12'	P.W.
	2 putts		2 putts	2 putts		5'		12'
						1 putt		

Previous all-time PGA tour 18-hole record

60, BY AL BROSCH, at Brackenridge Park Golf Course, San Antonio, Texas, in third round of 1951 Texas Open.

60, BY BILL NARY, at El Paso Country Club, El Paso, Texas, in third round of 1952 El Paso Open.

60, BY TED KROLL, at Brackenridge Park Golf Course, San Antonio, Texas, in third round of 1954 Texas Open.

60, BY WALLY ULRICH, at Cavalier Yacht and Country Club, Virginia Beach, Virginia, in second round of 1954 Virginia Beach Open.

60, BY TOMMY BOLT, at Wethersfield Country Club, Hartford, Conn., in second round of 1954 Insurance City Open.

60, BY MIKE SOUCHAK, at Brackenridge Park Golf Course, San Antonio, Texas, in first round of 1955 Texas Open.

60, BY SAM SNEAD, at Glen Lakes Country Club, Dallas, Texas, in second round of 1957 Dallas Open.

heading right for the center again, but left it about a foot short. It was a real letdown. The par felt like a bogey.

On the fifth hole, a 199-yard par 3, I hit a 4-iron 30 feet from the hole and almost made the putt but ran it about three feet past. I was kind of in shock over missing the record, and I remember thinking, "Don't miss this putt and ruin a good round." I didn't.

As I look back on it, trying to break the tour record of eight under for eight holes was the best thing that could have happened to me. If I had said, back on the 10th hole, that I was going to shoot for a 59, I would have choked and never made it. But going for that goal within the round took my mind off my eventual score and got me past the choking point.

After I made the three-footer for my second par in a row, I really had to talk to myself. The gallery had really picked up by then and there was a lot of confusion. I was getting a little confused myself. I didn't even know how many under par I was, and I was a little let down from missing the record under-par string.

Finally I thought, "Wait a minute, you've got something going here. Let's see how low you can shoot. Pull out the stops and go." That's completely out of character for me. Like most players, I have a tendency when I get five or six or seven under par to draw back a little, to start playing it safe and not take advantage of the birdie chances I have the rest of the round. It's sort of a built-in barrier, a governor or something. You don't want to get greedy and ruin what you already have. Johnny Miller used to overcome that barrier when he was shooting those hot rounds a few years ago. And on this day I was able to overcome it.

The sixth hole, my 15th, is a 388-yard par 4 on which most players hit a 3-wood so they won't go over a hill and end up with a downhill lie. I hit my 3-wood over the hill, farther than I had intended. But I hit a pitching wedge 13 feet from the hole and made it for birdie.

Now I'm starting to think. I'm 11 under par. The lowest score I had ever shot was 61, on La Cumbre Country Club, my home course in California, and I could break that. Then, about the time I realized that I could shoot 59, the gallery did too. They started yelling, "59! 59! 59!"

That's something I had never heard before . . . and may never hear again in seriousness. I hear it a lot, but usually when I'm teeing off or when I'm making the turn four over par, and sometimes it doesn't set too well. But the fans had it all figured out. With three holes to play, all I had to do was birdie two of them for 59.

The seventh hole at Colonial is a par 5, 564 yards long. I hit a good drive and a big 3-wood closer than I'd ever been to the green, then knocked a pitching wedge nine feet above the hole.

This green is only about 200 yards from the clubhouse, and there are stands erected around it. I learned later that all the players in the locker room had come out to watch, which is an almost unheard-of circumstance on our tour. And of course everybody else from the clubhouse came out, too.

When you are playing well, you see a break and you know it's right. I stroked the nine-footer, and it had gone about three feet off the putter when I knew I had made it. It may have been my greatest show of confidence in a long time, but I just turned around and watched the gallery. I knew I had made the putt and was just waiting for the reaction. When the ball went in the hole, the fans just exploded and shot out of the stands. It was a moment I will never forget.

I wasn't watching any leader boards during the round, but I guess everybody else was. I learned later that Ken Still, one of our veteran players and the world's greatest rooter in any sport, was over on the other nine paying more attention to my game than he was to his. Ken is the kind of guy who will watch two ants crossing the sidewalk and start pulling for the one that's behind. The fellows he was playing with told me afterward he was going nuts, running all over hunting for scoreboards to watch those red numbers go up after my name.

So now I needed one more birdie with two holes to play. I think everybody on the premises, except the other players still on the course, was watching me. The eighth hole, my 17th, is the hardest hole on the course, a 479-yard par 4. Usually we hit 2- or 3-irons for our second shots, and I have hit a wood on occasion, but on this day I hit a big drive and a 5-iron 20 feet short of the hole. I hit a pretty good putt, but it was left of the hole all the way, ending up less than a foot away.

So the stage was set for the last hole, and the gallery was charging over to the tee yelling, "59!" I think I floated over, my feet never touching the ground.

The ninth at Colonial is a 402-yarder, dogleg left, with a trap at the corner that is just big enough and far enough out that you usually can't get over it. I hit a really solid drive that was hooking a little bit, and I was a little worried about the ball carrying the trap. But it did, and once you carry the trap you get a bonus, because the ball gets around the corner and runs. The next two days I found out how big a drive I had hit—I hit what felt like exactly the same tee shot and didn't get to the middle of the trap.

As I was waiting for Stockton and McGee to hit their second shots, I was having a disagreement with Lee Lynch, my caddie, on the yardage remaining. I had 121 yards to the pin and he had 127. I can hit my pitching wedge 115 yards normally, and when I'm pumped up I can go to 120 if I have to. Usually, in a tense situation, you go with the shorter club and hit it full, because there is less chance for error. You stay away from half shots, because when you swing easily under pressure there is a tendency for your swing to get away from you.

But on this day I had so much control over the club and was hitting the ball so well that I didn't have any doubts I could hit a three-quarter 9-iron and pull it off. I told Lee, "I've got a chance here, and I don't want

After the final putt.

to hit the pitching wedge and leave it 30 feet short of the hole. The pin is on the back and I don't want that long uphill putt to get to it."

So I hit the easy 9, and I hit it just right. It ended up just to the left of the hole, about eight feet away.

Around the green everybody was going crazy—there was yelling and screaming and a lot of emotion in the air. McGee was on the front of the green facing the long putt I hadn't wanted, and he ran it three or four feet above the hole, leaving himself a tricky little downhiller. Stockton was about 25 feet away, and he putted up and holed out in a hurry. He knew he had missed the cut, and I'm sure he just wanted to get out of my way.

I knew if I made my putt there would be bedlam, so I asked McGee if he wanted to putt out. Jerry said, "No, you go ahead." Well, I wasn't going to ask him twice. I wanted to get my putt off. I had already circled it 10 times, it seemed. People said I didn't look very nervous, but I was. Still, I was nervous in a confident way. Sometimes you're so nervous you have the feeling you're not going to be able to shake the ball off the putter. But my stroke felt good, and I was positive I wasn't going to choke and not be able to get the putter through.

My putt was a little bit uphill with a slight left-to-right break. It was one of those putts that I knew where I wanted to play it the instant I looked at it—about an inch outside the hole on the left. My main concern was that because of the grainy Bermuda green I might leave it short.

I hit the putt and I didn't leave it short. It just dove right in the center of the cup. And all hell broke loose. Everybody was jumping up and down, including Jerry McGee. You would have thought he had shot the 59.

Finally, after everybody calmed down a little, Jerry went back and made his putt. Afterward, I asked him why he didn't go ahead and putt when I gave him the chance. He said, "If I missed that putt, I didn't want to feel responsible for you missing yours." In other words, he didn't want to set up any negative patterns. I thought that was pretty nice of him under the circumstances. As it turned out, he finished second in the tournament, so that could have been a pretty crucial putt.

I didn't realize at the moment exactly what I had done. It sounded great to shoot 59, but I didn't know that nobody had ever broken 60 in PGA Tour competition. I think I finally realized the enormity of it when I walked into the press room and got a long, standing ovation.

Once I came out of my daze, I began to appreciate my accomplishment. I had hit every fairway and every green. Surprisingly enough, I probably have hit the ball better on occasion. At least I have hit my irons closer to the hole, especially when I won the Tournament Players Championship at Colonial Country Club in Fort Worth in 1975. But I never have had a better putting round. I took only 23 putts, and the closest birdie putt I had was five feet. I made an eight-footer and a nine-footer on my back nine, but every other birdie putt ranged from 12 to 45 feet.

I've been asked if playing preferred lies helped my score, and I can't really answer the question. I did move the ball some, although I normally don't like to improve my lies. But what grass there was was new and tight, and it was hard to find a place to get a really good lie. The cut score the previous year had been 144, and it was 144 in 1977. The next best score to mine was 65, so playing preferred lies didn't seem to help that much.

One of the oddities of my round is that I violated a cardinal rule all the big-time pros follow, which is to use fresh golf balls throughout the round. Most tour players use six balls during the round, usually alternating them every hole. I usually start out with the intention of using three balls, playing one for six holes and then changing. There are various reasons for this, having to do with a ball's ability to recover its shape after being struck and its durability over a number of holes.

All of that is definitely science and not myth, but I'm not sure how much it means, because I used one ball for the entire round. I had started out with my usual intention of switching, but once the ball started going in the hole for me I decided to stick with it until something went wrong. Nothing did.

Today, the ball is in the Hall of Fame at Pinehurst, N.C. It is suspended in a big glass case with a blue velvet background, lights playing on it. It looks like the Hope diamond. As far as I'm concerned, on that day in 1977, it was.

Despite the 59, my most difficult accomplishment of the week was coming back to win the tournament. I mean, you are supposed to win the tournament when you shoot 59, right? That gave me a six-shot lead at the halfway mark. I shot another 72 in the third round and was still three shots ahead. But I double-bogeyed the fourth hole on the final day, shot 38 for the first nine holes and at that point was two shots behind Gary Player. About that time I convinced myself I had to forget the 59 and get back to reality. I shot 32 coming in for a 70 and won the tournament by three strokes. I felt like I had won two tournaments that week.

Of course, I will be the subject of some golf trivia questions as the years go by. For example, who shot 15 under par in a 72-hole tournament without a round in the 60s? Or, who is the only man in one year to shoot in the 50s, 60s, 70s and 80s? Within two weeks of my 59 I shot 80 in the Western Open at Butler National in Chicago. I could have added to that trivia' record, too, because· about a month later I shot an 85 in Canada and thought about trying for 90—but my pride wouldn't let me.

The longer I think about it, the more I can credit the 59 to the fact that I was able to maintain my tempo throughout the round. The more birdies I made and the more the pressure built, the better I hit the ball. This was because ! had that positive swing thought to work with. I also had the positive putting thought, which is why my putting held up under the pressure.

That's why it is so important to constantly review your fundamentals, a subject we are going to pursue later in this book. No matter how many pars or birdies you make at the start, if your swing is flawed and you don't have confidence in it, your game eventually will fall apart. But if your fundamentals are solid and you know it, your tempo will be good and stay good, no matter how much pressure is put on it.

The development and maintenance of that good tempo is what the rest of this book is all about. I can't promise you that good tempo will let you shoot 59, but it surely will help you play better and more consistently.

"59! 59! 59!"

TEMPO: WHAT IT IS AND HOW TO GET IT

The tempo I had working during my 59 round is what every golfer searches for. It is the ingredient that ties the swing together and produces the timing that is so essential to effective ball-striking.

Because we are human, tempo can vary from day to day. I wish I always could swing as I did that day in Memphis, but I can't. However, you *can* make your tempo more consistent, which means that your timing and your game will be better and more stable each time out. All you need is an understanding of what produces tempo in the golf swing and the patience to work to achieve it.

Let me clear up the confusion many golfers have over the difference between tempo and timing. The dictionary defines tempo as "rate of motion or activity; pace." In other words, tempo is the speed of your swing. That speed will vary with each individual. The best rule for finding your ideal tempo is to *swing at the maximum speed at which you can control your body and the club*.

Timing is the sequence of motion, the order in which things happen during your swing. When you have good timing, the clubhead arrives at the ball traveling at peak speed and aiming straight at the target. The ball then flies long and true. When this happens, you know your timing was right. You also know your tempo was good, because tempo and timing—separate and distinct factors that they are—become inseparable when you swing a golf club.

Timing, especially, depends on good tempo. You must give yourself enough time during the swing for everything to happen as it should. If you try to hit the ball too hard and swing too fast, your swing will go out of control and you will ruin the correct sequence of motion by the parts of your body.

By the same token, if your timing or sequence is out of whack, it precludes a good tempo. Poor fundamentals that result in poor positions during the swing usually cause a player to swing too fast and destroy any chance he or she has of catching the ball squarely.

This is what happens to most players. It is my firm belief—and the premise of this book—that good tempo is created by sound fundamentals.

I break down the fundamentals into four areas, and we'll spend the next four chapters examining those. But before we do, let me talk a little about the importance of good tempo and how achieving it will lead to better shots and lower scores for you.

The relationship between tempo and timing once was neatly expressed by a friend of mine named Dave Evans, who was an engineering genius and an avid student of the golf swing. He contended, and I have always agreed, that *you have only one fast moment in each swing, and you had better use it where it counts.*

That simply means that if you use your one fast moment too soon (very seldom, if ever, does it come too late), it won't be there when you need it as you swing through the impact area. If you take the club away from the ball too fast, or if you start down from the top of your swing too fast, all you can do from there is decelerate. Not only will you lose clubhead speed and distance, you also will lose accuracy, because those too-fast movements early in the swing will throw you out of control and keep you from striking the ball squarely.

Even the pros have the problem of swinging too quickly at the wrong time. The adrenaline starts pumping under pressure and the swing starts racing. The tour players know very well the value of slowing things down. Jack Nicklaus says that when he wants to hit the ball farther, he takes the club back more slowly. Tom Watson's dramatic improvement began when he slowed his swing down a little at the top and greatly improved his tempo. During his great 1973 season, when he won the British Open and six other tournaments, Tom Weiskopf said he was doing everything more slowly—not only swinging but walking and even brushing his teeth more slowly. He knew instinctively that the pace of your swing can be a reflection of the pace of your habits in life and your approach to golf. By slowing everything else down, he could better slow down his swing.

If *your* swing is too fast, too soon, there are some keys that will help you slow down. First, think of trying to strike the ball before you reach your maximum speed. Feel that your one fast moment in your swing is coming after you strike the ball. That probably won't happen. Centrifugal force and the generation of clubhead speed as a result of good timing won't let it happen. What *will* happen is that the fast moment will occur at the right time, as the club is sweeping through the impact area. For most players, who are used to unleashing the fast moment too soon, it will just seem that it's happening late in the swing. If you have been swinging too fast too early, it will feel as if you are accelerating through the ball, sending the clubhead speeding out toward the target. This feeling of forward movement through the shot will promote greater accuracy because it keeps the clubhead going down the target line longer.

I've emphasized swinging more slowly and easily, fully realizing that distance comes from clubhead speed. But there is really no conflict. In the first place, I'm talking about swinging more slowly and easily during the stages of the swing that you can control, the backswing and the start of the forward swing. By *thinking* of swinging more easily from the start, your muscles will be more relaxed and supple, which means you actually can swing the club faster when you need to than if they were tight. By thinking of swinging more slowly, you will save your fast moment for the right time and will strike the ball more squarely. As George Bayer, one of the longest hitters ever, once said, "If you want to hit the ball farther, don't hit it harder, hit it better."

How many times have you told yourself to "swing easy" and proceeded to knock the ball 20 yards farther than normal? I often play better when I'm tired. And there's an adage on tour that you watch out for the player who is sick. I had the 24-hour flu during a tournament in Las Vegas one year. All night I figured there was no way I was going to play the next day. But in the morning I felt a little bit stronger. I hit one practice shot before I teed off, and I had my best round of the tournament. I just felt so bad I had to swing easier, and I hit better shots because of it. Yet we can't seem to convince ourselves that this is going to work every time.

Believe me, it will. To prove it to yourself conclusively, seek out a professional in your area who has one of the electronic swing machines that measure clubhead speed and ball carry. You'll find that the more relaxed you are during the swing, the greater your clubhead speed will be through the impact zone. Your ball carry also will be greater, because you are striking the ball more squarely and on the proper angle.

Don't, however, mistake an easy swing for a patty-cake swing. There must be power and force in the golf swing for it to be effective. When I get everything collected in good position at the top and get started down properly, I have a firm feeling of acceleration, of power, as I swing through the shot. There is no sudden burst of power. I don't think you can delay the application of clubhead speed and suddenly turn it on at the bottom of the swing. Rather, there is a gradual buildup of centrifugal force on the clubhead until it is, hopefully, traveling at maximum speed when it contacts the ball.

I've been told my swing looks effortless. Well, I feel a lot of effort going into it, but I suspect that what I feel is the power created by that centrifugal force, by everything happening in the correct sequence throughout the swing.

I do know that I am putting a lot less effort into the swing than a lot of amateurs I see. I've tried in clinics to emulate them by taking the club back as fast as I can and swinging as fast as I can through the rest of the swing. I get out of breath. So, compared to the person who is making a lot of bad moves, my swing *is* effortless. This is particularly true as I

Backswing

.90 Seconds

Change of direction

.24 Seconds

To impact

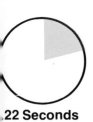

.22 Seconds

Follow-through

.52 Seconds

Swing it slowly to the top

This comparative breakdown shows the time Geiberger spends in the various stages of his swing. The 24 sequence photos represent an exact ratio of the 94 frames, shot at 50 frames per second, that it takes Geiberger to make this shot with a driver. Of the total 1.88 seconds required to complete the swing, he spends .9 of a second, or almost half the time, from takeaway to the top of his backswing. Note how slowly the club moves away from the ball in the initial stages, setting the pattern for his tempo throughout the swing. Geiberger spends .24 of a second in a virtually motionless position at the top while the club is changing direction. Once this is accomplished, the swing accelerates gradually but dramatically, and it takes only .22 of a second to reach impact. From there he moves into a smooth follow-through that takes .52 of a second to reach completion. These pictures corroborate Geiberger's contention that you should swing slower and easier during the stages you can control, on the backswing and at the start of the forward swing.

move from the shorter to the longer clubs. Most amateurs swing progressively harder as the club gets longer. On the other hand, I like to feel I'm swinging my 2-iron at the same pace I swing my 9-iron. The length and loft of the club will provide all the distance I need. I don't need to help it with extra effort. And that's a good thought for you.

I'm often asked to put a percentage figure on how hard I swing. I'm not sure, but I know it's not 100 percent of my strength. Some professionals think they approach an all-out swing. Tom Watson says he swings the driver at 98 percent of his capability, sometimes 100 percent. But I can't do that. If I tried to go 100 percent, my swing would fall apart. Sam Snead says he swings at about 85 percent most of the time, and that might be pretty close for me, too.

As I said earlier, an individual's strength has a lot to do with how hard he or she can swing. Obviously, the stronger you are, the better you can control a faster swing. Still, I always remember that Dr. Gary Wiren of the PGA once said, "A golfer needs to get stronger, not so he can swing harder but so he can swing easier."

One thing is fact—the more fundamentally sound your swing is, the harder you can swing on those occasions when you need a little extra distance. But if your fundamentals are not sound and you get out of position, there comes a feeling of insecurity and impatience that speeds up your swing at the wrong time and ruins your shot.

I divide the fundamentals of the swing into four categories—grip, setup, use of the left arm and use of the legs. If that sounds simple, it's because my philosophy always has been to simplify the game of golf as much as possible.

Years ago, as a teenager, I realized I was not going to be a big, strong player. I'm tall and gangly now, and I was really skinny as a kid. A Charles Atlas I was not. I was raised in Sacramento, Calif., until I was 15 years old, and I got some very good advice from Bus Pendleton, a professional there. He made me realize that the simpler my swing, the better I was going to be, because I wasn't going to be able to rely on pure strength. Players with strong hands and arms are better able to compensate for errors in their swings. But when my fundamentals break down, I'm not strong enough to compensate. So I've always tried to keep my swing simple, adhering to those fundamentals. Unless you have more strength and talent than most, I recommend that you do the same. The closer you stay to your fundamentals, the better, more consistently and longer you will play.

For years I have listened to Jack Nicklaus and other tour professionals tell me about how they tear down their swings and start over when things are going badly. For a long time I thought that might be very risky for most amateurs. Obviously a Jack Nicklaus is able to do it, because he is technically so well-grounded in the fundamentals of his swing and is such a fine athlete that he can work successfully with all of the intricacies. But after spending more and more time working with amateurs in clinics and outings and working with my sons, I've come to the conclusion that anybody can do the same thing Nicklaus does provided he or she has some simple rules to follow. If you can refer to a one-two-three-four series of checkpoints, it makes it much easier to build a solid swing and to rescue your game when your swing goes bad—as it does occasionally with all of us. If you don't have a dozen or more things to think about, if you have only four sound fundamentals to check off, you can escape the "paralysis by analysis" problem that plagues most golfers.

After we discuss my four fundamental areas in the following chapters, we'll talk about how to blend them properly to achieve good tempo. Please give the fundamentals careful attention before you move on to later chapters. Even if you have played golf for some time, it is essential to improving your tempo to clearly understand the role of the grip, setup, left arm and legs in the swing.

After you have read the next four chapters, to prove to yourself the validity of what I say, go to the practice area at your course or to a driving range at a busy time and watch the ball-beaters there. Focus on the fundamental areas I've described and observe how most players abuse them—with disastrous results. Conversely, watch how a good player— your club professional, maybe, or a top amateur—executes all four of these fundamentals correctly.

Please understand that I'm not saying the game is easy. There are many complexities within each of the fundamental areas, and I'm going to deal with them in this book. But all of the complex movements in the swing will happen naturally if your grip and posture are correct and if you adhere to some simple concepts during the swing. Your tempo immediately gets better and the game quickly becomes much easier.

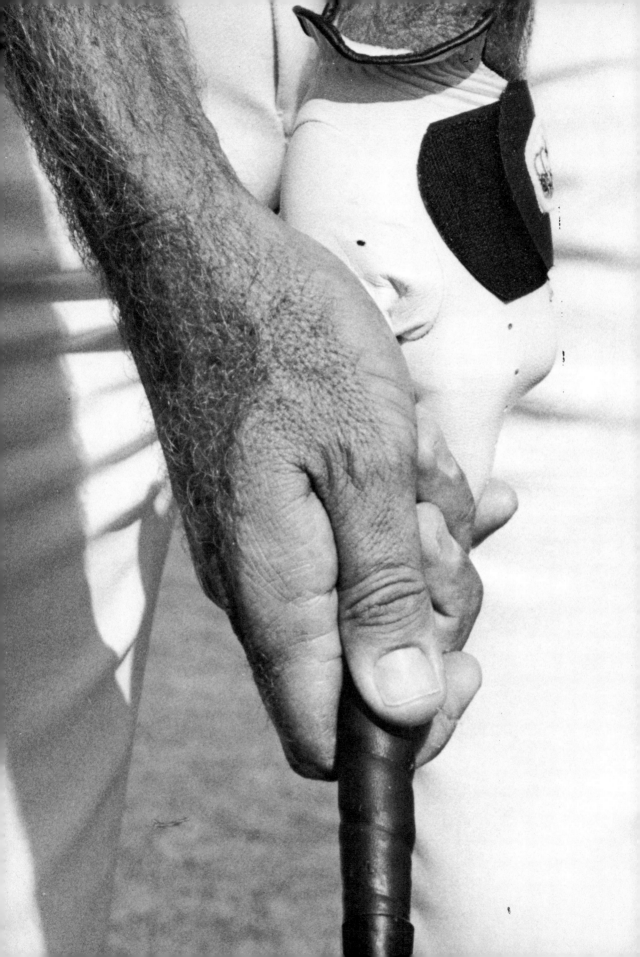

FUNDAMENTAL No. 1: GRIP

People get bored hearing and reading about the grip. It's just not a very exciting subject. I also suspect there is a built-in resistance to grip talk among golfers who have played for any length of time. A grip change is the most difficult alteration to make in a person's approach to the swing, and they just don't want to go through the discomfort.

Well, I'm sorry about that, but if you are going to be a good player, you will have to pay some attention to your grip. The grip may be the key to the golf swing, because *it tells the clubface where to go.* Your hands are your only connection to the club, and if that connection is faulty, you have to come up with some patchwork to make the club work properly. You are then covering up one fault with another. Sooner or later—usually sooner—that kind of compensation is going to catch up with you, your tempo will be destroyed and your swing will come to grief.

That being the case, let's take a look at how to get your hands on the club properly.

I was very impressed with a clinic I once saw given by Dr. Gary Wiren of the PGA. One of the things Gary pointed out was that your hands should be placed on the club the way they hang naturally at your side. Try this out for yourself. Bend slightly from your hips and let your arms hang in front of you. Note where the back of your left hand and the palm of your right hand face in relation to an imaginary target. That's the natural position in which your arms and hands hang. They are going to want to return there at the bottom of your swing, just when you are striking the ball. So if you make any radical departure from that position when you put your hands on the club, you are asking for trouble.

The ideal position from which to swing the club would have the palms facing each other, the back of the left hand and the palm of the right hand facing approximately toward your target. This position gives you the best chance of returning the clubface square to the target at impact.

The assumption here, and throughout the remainder of the instruction in this book, is that you are right-handed. (If you are a left-hander,

Place hands on club as they hang

Ideally, your hands should be placed on the golf club in the same position they are as you stand erect with your arms hanging naturally and relaxed, within the other guidelines discussed in this chapter.

simply reverse the left/right designations.)

If your hands don't happen to hang naturally in that palms-facing or "neutral" position, don't worry about it. You may have to make some modification in your hand position to accommodate the handle of the club and to set the club properly on the ground. But the closer you can come to the palms-facing position while still letting your hands hang in their natural position, the better off you will be.

Your left hand is the primary connection to the club. Whatever the left hand does, the clubface will do. If the left hand turns over, the clubface will turn over right with it. So you want to grip the club in the *palm* of the left hand. That gives you the firmness you need to best control the club.

So the left hand should be placed on the club with the handle running diagonally across the palm, from the base of the forefinger up under the heel pad (see p. 38-39). Let your left arm and hand hang, and place your hand on the club in that manner, in as natural a position as possible. Close your fingers and thumb around the club. The left thumb should be resting slightly to the right side of the club handle, but only slightly, because the left thumb helps support the club at the top of the swing, and the closer to center it is on the shaft, the squarer the club is likely to be at the top.

The V formed by your thumb and forefinger can point anywhere between your right shoulder and your chin. That depends on how your hand was hanging. If the V points anywhere outside that range, you should make an adjustment to get it within those boundaries.

I do a lot of teaching in clinics and outings that I give around the world, and I play with amateurs in pro-am events almost every week. I see a lot of bad left-hand grips. But I see an incredibly larger percentage of bad *right-hand* grips.

To me, the reason is relatively obvious. There's an old saying that when you first go into the army they issue you fatigues, boots and a cold, and you spend your entire army career getting rid of that cold. When you first start to play golf, you are issued clubs, spikes and a slice, and you spend your life getting rid of that slice.

Unfortunately, most players try to get rid of the slice by grabbing the club in the palm of the right hand and cranking the hand to the right or underneath the shaft, which is the last place you want it.

That right-hand position gives you a feeling of security. You are right-handed; that's the strong hand, and now it's in control of the club. The problem is that you are adding a whole bunch of new faults to the fault that you already have. You still have the slice problem in your swing, and you have created new problems because you are going to have trouble getting that right hand and the clubface back to the position in which you want it at impact.

With the right hand turned well to the right, you will tend to close the clubface as you swing it back. So when you reach the top of your swing and start back down, if you make a normal turn of the body and let your arms and hands swing naturally, the clubface will close even more and you'll produce a big, diving hook.

After a few of those, you will be trying to manipulate your hands to get the clubface square. You probably will be raising up and falling back at impact in an effort to avoid that hook. In any event, there is no way you can take a nice, free swing through the ball. The right hand is in such a dominant position that it overpowers the left hand, arm and side. That's the last thing you want to have happen.

The answer is simply to place the right hand on the club in as close to its natural position as possible, keeping in mind the palms-facing guideline, and to hold the club with the *fingers* of the hand, not the palm.

With your left hand on the club, the left thumb will rest in the channel formed by the heel and thumb pads of your right hand. In the basic Vardon or overlapping grip that I and most players use, the ring finger of your right hand rests snugly against the forefinger of your left while your right little finger overlaps or is crooked around that forefinger (see p. 38 39). Your right forefinger should be a bit triggered, the right thumb resting against the top left side of the handle. The V formed by the right thumb and forefinger should be pointing somewhere between your chin and your right shoulder, the same as the left V. Ideally, both V's will point in about the same direction, but again that will depend to some extent on how your hands hang naturally.

A good way to check your right-hand position is to assume your grip with both hands and take your address position next to a mirror. Look at yourself from the side. There should be a slight arch to your right wrist. If

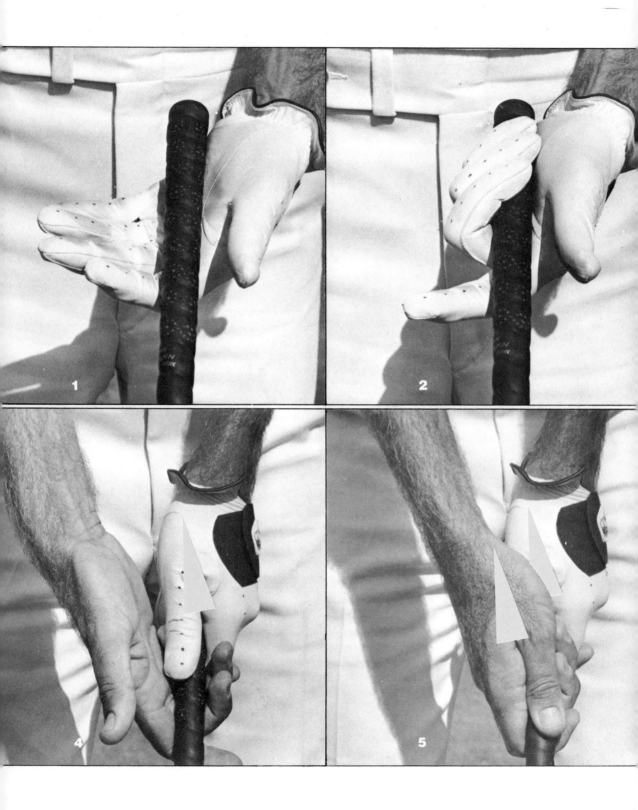

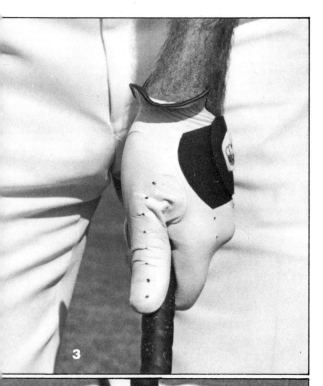

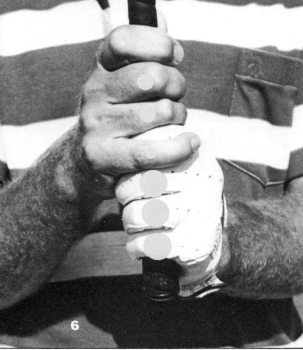

How to assume your grip

The club should be held in the palm of the left hand, the handle running diagonally from the base of the forefinger up under the heel pad (1). Close your last three fingers (2) around the club, then close the forefinger and thumb (3), the thumb resting just slightly to the right side of the handle and the V formed by your thumb and forefinger pointing anywhere between your right shoulder and your chin. The club is held in the fingers of the right hand (4), the ring finger of the right resting snugly against the forefinger of the left and the little finger overlapping the left forefinger or crooked around it. The right forefinger is triggered and the right thumb rests against the top left side of the handle (5), the V pointing approximately in the same direction as the V of the left. The pressure is in the last three fingers of the left and the middle two fingers of the right, with the overlapped little finger of the right also exerting some pressure (6).

there is not, the right hand is turned too far under the shaft.

The grip that you now have formed lets the two hands work together and complement each other during the swing. The club is firmly in the palm of the left hand, which controls the club and pulls it through the swing. It rests in the fingers of the right, allowing you to apply the power that comes from the right side and still keep the clubface square, because you are not overpowering the left or turning the club with the right hand.

The arms now can swing and rotate freely back and through the swing, and the clubface will stay square to the swing arc and return square to the target at impact without any manipulation of the hands. And don't worry if the position feels "weak" to you or if you feel you will slice. We'll get rid of the slice with correction in your alignment or swing, which is undoubtedly where the problem lies anyway.

As for grip pressure, I subscribe to the theory that the swing should be controlled with the last three fingers of the left hand, so that's where most of the pressure should be. In the right hand, I feel most of the pressure in the ring and index fingers, although the overlapped little finger is applying some pressure also. The right thumb and forefinger are basically resting on the club, applying only enough pressure to give me some support at the top of the swing.

How much pressure? A good guide is to set the club on the ground; take your grip; then lift the clubhead slightly off the ground with your left hand alone, using only enough strength to hold it there. That doesn't require much pressure, does it? Probably a lot less than you are used to, because if you are like most amateurs, you grip the club far too tightly.

By exerting only enough pressure with your left hand to hold the club off the ground, you can keep your arms relaxed. At this point, the right hand is just resting on the club, going along for the ride. As soon as you start gripping too tightly, tension creeps in and ties up your swing.

Your thought now should be to maintain this light grip pressure throughout the swing. Don't be afraid of the club slipping from your grasp during the swing. Your grip will tighten instinctively as you swing, but if you think of keeping your grip pressure constant, it will tighten only enough to accommodate the weight and force of the swing, and you will be able to stay relatively free of tension.

Here are some further grip tips:

• Always align your clubface to your target before you assume your grip. If you don't, you are liable to adjust the clubface alignment simply by turning your hands, which will provide you with an unpleasant surprise when you get back to impact. I don't take my final grip until I'm virtually ready to start my swing. The club just kind of sits in my fingers until then. This helps me stay relaxed in my fingers, hands and arms.

• The size of the grips on your clubs is important. Ideally, the tips of the ring and index fingers of your left hand should just touch the thumb pad when you are gripping the club tightly enough to control it. If the fingers are digging into the pad, your grips are too small. If they aren't touching the thumb pad, the grips are too big and you will lose feel and inhibit your hand and forearm rotation. If you have to go one way or the other, it's usually better that your grips be too small, especially if you tend to slice the ball. Hopefully, you will find a professional who can fit you properly.

• When you take your left-hand grip, choke down far enough on the club so the butt rests just outside the heel pad of your left hand. If the butt rests against the heel pad, your grip will not be as firm and the club will have more tendency to flop around during the swing. You also can raise a callus on your hand.

If you have played golf for some time and this chapter has convinced you to change your grip, please be patient when you do. Just as your bad grip feels good to you now, so a good grip will be comfortable *when you get used to it.* So don't panic when you feel uncomfortable and don't play as well for a while.

Finally, if you have a severe grip adjustment to make, do it gradually, getting used to each slight change before you make another. It will take time and perseverance, but it will be worth it to you in better play.

RECAP—GRIP

● Your grip, especially the grip in your left hand, tells your clubface where to go.

● Place your hands on the club in as close to a palms-facing position as you can while letting them hang as naturally as possible.

● Grip in the palm of the left hand and in the fingers of the right.

● The V's formed by your thumbs and forefingers should point somewhere between your chin and your right shoulder and should point generally in the same direction, depending on your individual characteristics.

● Pressure should be applied with the last three fingers of the left hand, the middle two fingers of the right.

● Apply only enough pressure with the left hand to lift the club off the ground. At address, the right hand is simply resting on the club.

FUNDAMENTAL No. 2: SETUP

When we discuss "setup," we're actually talking about three separate elements involved in addressing the ball—posture, aim and alignment. Posture has to do with the position of the parts of your body. Aim is simply where the clubface is pointing. Alignment is the relationship of your body to the clubface and target line.

I don't know that any one of these elements is more important than another. All are vital. Good posture enables you to make a "natural" swing, or as close to a natural swing as you can make in what is basically an unnatural game. It makes it possible for you to swing without really thinking about the mechanics of the swing. If the parts of the body are in the right place, everything happens more easily and correctly during the swing.

Good posture allows your legs to work properly, your shoulders to turn on the correct plane and your arms to swing in a free and relaxed manner. Good posture creates good tempo because it relaxes you. It gives you the confidence that you are in good position and can just make a natural turn and swing.

Correct aim and alignment, of course, allow you to make that good swing in the right direction, so you can strike the ball where you want it to go.

Posture

Good posture, unfortunately, is not natural or easily acquired. In my clinics and outings I see an unbelievable variety of postures, most of them bad. I spend more time getting people into position to make a decent swing than on anything else.

If you give a club to a person who has never played golf before, I'll guarantee he will bend over and reach too far for the ball, stiffening the legs in the process; or he will stand too erect, bending too much in the legs.

Let's take a look at what these poor postures—common among all

Incorrect body tilt causes faulty knee flex

If your upper body is too erect (left), you must squat too much with your legs. If you are bent over too much (right), your legs will stiffen. Either fault causes an inability to use the legs properly and results in tension and compensations that ruin tempo.

golfers, not just beginners—do to a swing.

If you are bent over too much and your legs are stiff, you obviously cannot use your legs well, which causes your hands to take over. You are likely to fall off balance during your swing. You will create a lot of tempo-destroying tension because you are reaching too far for the ball.

If your upper body is too erect at address, you have to squat too much with the legs to get the club down to the ball. This also restricts the movement of your legs. It makes your swing too flat, causing your club to fall below its ideal plane and forcing you to jam the club back into the ball primarily with your hands. Again, your swing speeds up and your tempo goes out the window.

I find one of the major causes of poor posture is an inability to relate to correct ball position. I am repeatedly asked, "How far away should I stand from the ball?"

As far as I'm concerned, that's going at it backwards. Your posture should not be determined by where the ball is. You let your posture determine where the ball should be played.

Individual postures must vary, of course, because physical characteristics vary. But every golfer, tall or short, broad or slender, can work

within the same concept and can find his ideal posture by following these simple guidelines:

● Stand erect, legs straight, arms hanging at your sides, your feet about shoulder-width apart.

● Flex your knees slightly, just enough to break the stiffness.

● Bend forward from the hips, keeping your back straight, and as you do, stick your derriere out. Bend enough that your arms can hang straight down and clear of your body as you swing them gently back and forth in front of you, much as an elephant swings his trunk.

You are now in a basically correct posture. Simple, isn't it? Now repeat the process, this time with a club in your left hand. When you are bent forward so your arms are hanging naturally, assume your grip on the club and place the clubhead properly soled on the ground. That's how far away the ball should be played with that club. The distance will vary with different clubs, of course, but if you first acquire a feeling for the correct posture, you will almost automatically set up the correct distance away.

There are some refinements and some problem areas to be aware of in working with your posture.

Bend from the hips until arms hang freely

To find your correct posture, flex your knees slightly and bend from the hips until your arms hang freely (left). Then assume the same posture with a club in your hands (right). From this position, with the club properly soled, you will be standing the correct distance from the ball.

45

Set lower body properly

Keep weight on the inside of your right foot and evenly distributed on your left, with both knees thrust slightly toward the target (left), your upper body set behind your lower body. Your weight should be set toward the balls of your feet (right). With your back straight, your derriere sticking out and your legs slightly flexed, you should feel a slight tension or stretching in the back of your legs.

Achieving the correct upper body tilt prevents the arms from stretching too far for the ball or from being jammed so close to the body that they cannot swing. Just as with the hands in the grip, the natural hanging position is best for the arms because they will seek to return to that position during the swing. If everything is in order at address, it will be a lot easier to get back to the correct position at impact.

You also will have taken a big step toward establishing a good swing plane, which simply means the vertical angle at which the club is swung in relation to the ground. The swing plane is determined by your shoulder turn and the swinging of your arms. The arms actually swing on a higher or more vertical plane than the shoulders, but obviously there is a relationship.

Unless some terribly unnatural effort is made, the shoulders will turn around the spine. That being the case, it's easy to see how your spine angle or body tilt can affect your swing plane. If your spine is too erect, your shoulder turn and swing plane will be too flat, like a baseball player's. If you are bent over too much and your spine is too tilted, your shoulder turn and swing will be too upright. But if you bend from the hips so that your arms can swing free of your body, your spine angle and shoulder turn will be right for a good swing plane. It's as simple as that.

Be sure that when you bend, you do not slouch. Keep your spine straight and just let your shoulders and arms relax and hang naturally. Don't let your head droop or it will interfere with your arm swing. Keep your neck in line with the tilt of your spine.

As important as your upper body position is in good posture, getting your lower body properly set is equally so.

Your weight should be toward the balls of your feet, because your legs are more mobile from that position. The weight should not be on your toes and definitely not on your heels, because your leg movement is then inhibited. When I'm playing well, my right heel tends to be slightly off the ground as I begin my backswing. I'm told that Ben Hogan did this too, which may be the only golfing characteristic we ever had in common.

Where your weight rests is closely tied in with how much you bend your knees. The more flexed your knees, the more your weight tends to go back toward the heels and the more your upper body is thrown erect. In fact, if you will reverse the first two steps of the procedure I gave you—bend forward while keeping your legs stiff, then flex your knees until your weight goes to the balls of your feet—you'll find you have about the right amount of flex.

You also don't want *too* much flex because it takes away from the firmness you need in your legs during the swing. I was once criticized by Bob Toski for having too much knee flex, and I suspect that sometimes I do. I'm tall and I tend to want to get closer to the ground by bending my knees instead of bending from the hips. When that happens, my legs don't work as well as I want them to. They get too loose and rubbery.

Another check to see that your legs are ready to operate and your posture is correct—if you keep your back straight while you bend from the hips and stick out your derriere, you'll feel a stretching in the back of your legs. It's a good feeling that wakes up the dormant muscles.

My weight is pretty equally distributed between both feet on all shots, although it tends to go a little more toward my left with the shorter clubs. I also feel the weight should be set toward the inside of your right foot and evenly distributed on your left. It should definitely not be toward the outsides of the feet. I used to pinch my knees in, which kept the weight to the insides of the feet. I still do that with the right knee, but now I thrust my left knee a bit more toward the target.

As a rule of thumb, your right foot should be set square or perpendicular to your target line, while the left foot should toe out slightly to make it easier to turn the lower body on the forward swing.

Because you want your head behind the ball at impact, for reasons

9-iron

Driver

Stance, ball position vary with club

With the 9-iron (left), your stance should be relatively narrow. The longer the club, the more you should widen your stance. Geiberger's stance with a driver (right) is not quite as wide as his shoulders. Yours should be wide enough to match your physical proportions and accommodate the speed of your swing. With an iron, the ball should be positioned two or three inches inside the left heel. With the driver, it should be played off the left heel or instep.

I'll discuss later, you also want it there at address. In other words, your head will be to the right of the ball if you are a right-handed player.

Mainly, this is accomplished by that slight thrust of your legs toward the target and by the fact that your right hand is on the club below your left. This sets your right side a bit lower than your left and tilts your upper body slightly to the right. Conversely, it puts the left side higher and the left arm into a position from which it can control the swing.

Ball position and stance width are interrelated. With my irons, I actually play the ball from the same spot every time. I simply widen my stance for the longer clubs. With the wedge, for which my feet are set less than a foot apart, I'll play the ball just forward of the center of my stance—I would recommend never playing the ball back of center except for special shots. That puts it two or three inches back of (to the right of) the inside of my left heel. As the clubs get longer, I'll leave the ball in the same place relative to my left heel and just widen my stance.

A good way to find your best ball position is to take practice swings with several irons and note where the divot marks appear. Since you want to strike the ball before you hit the ground, spot the ball just behind or to the right of the divot mark.

You can move the ball a bit forward or closer to your left heel for the fairway woods, but not too far forward, because you still strike those with a slightly descending arc. With a driver, with the ball on a tee, you want to catch it with a level blow or slightly on the upswing, later in the circle or arc of the swing. So position the ball farther ahead, about off your left heel or instep.

My stance, which is narrower than most, is not quite as wide as my shoulders—measured from the insides of my heels—with the driver and gets progressively narrower with the shorter clubs. Yours may differ slightly. With each club, you want your stance wide enough to accommodate the force of your swing, so you can stay in balance. But you don't want it so wide that you restrict the movement of your legs. Those should be your guidelines in finding the best stance width for you.

Aim

Now that you are in position to hit the ball, you want to hit it in the right direction. To do that, you have to aim it. Simple as that sounds—and it really is simple—it probably gives golfers more trouble than any other phase of the game.

To have any chance of getting the ball started on the line you want, you must first get the clubface straight with that line, then get the parts of your body straight with the clubface. Let's start with the clubface.

In fact, that's the first thing you do—aim the clubface. Most golfers who have aiming problems do so because they line up their bodies first, then try to get the clubface aimed. Because they probably have lined their bodies up at the target, their clubfaces are going to be aimed to the right of the target, and right away they're in trouble.

So first aim the clubface on the line on which you want the ball to start. Work in practice toward acquiring a sense of what a squarely aimed clubface looks like. There are some devices you can use. Scratch a line in the turf in the direction of your target. Or place a club or a board parallel to your target line and just outside it. Then be sure your clubface is set square or perpendicular to the line when you address the ball. Always relate the position of the clubface to the target as well as the line so you can learn to identify a square clubface when you get on the course and can't use the artificial aids.

One "device" you *can* use on the course is the intermediate spot, which is simply some identifiable mark or object on your target line a few feet in front of your ball. Pick out the spot from behind your ball, then aim your clubface at the spot instead of your target. The theory is that it's easier to aim at a close-by object than one in the distance. You also get a

Set body parallel to line of play

After aiming your clubface at your target, set your feet, knees, hips, shoulders and eyes on a line parallel to your target line.

little better idea of the line on which you want to swing the club.

Alignment

Once you have the clubface properly aimed, align your body squarely with it. That means you set your feet, knees, hips and shoulders on a line that is *perpendicular* to the clubface or *parallel* to your line of play. Again, you can use clubs, boards or lines in practice to develop a sense of square body alignment.

It's important to get all those parts of your body I mentioned set up squarely or parallel to your line of play. Otherwise your swing will be going in a different direction. But I think the most important parts to get properly aligned are your *eyes*. Unless your eyes are parallel to the line of play, it's almost impossible to aim or align correctly.

Bud Palmer, the former basketball player and sportscaster, asked me for a lesson one time. I could see right away that for a big guy and a good athlete, he had a very weak swing. It didn't have any zip, because he took the club so far inside the target line on his backswing that he was just struggling to get it on line coming through. He would come over the top (spinning to the outside or toward the target line with the right shoulder) and he didn't have any power left by the time he got to the ball.

I tried to get him to take the club back straight, but he was having trouble. He had a hook grip, his hands turned too far to the right, and his hands were way too far ahead of the ball at address. Whenever I could get him to move his hands back where they belonged, he could take the club back straight. But his hands kept wanting to creep back ahead.

Finally, I realized Bud had his head tilted to the right, which tilted his eyes and aimed them to the right. It was interesting to see that his club-face aligned every time with the side of his face—aiming to the right. Because of the way his eyes were setting, that looked square to him.

That also caused his hands to go forward and caused him to take the club back inside. He thought he was taking it straight back. From that far inside he had to come over the top on the forward swing. Once he did that, his right arm was taking over, overpowering and breaking down the extension of his left side.

That entire chain reaction of unfortunate events was caused by improper alignment of the eyes. I tell you this lengthy story to impress on you the importance of aligning them correctly.

Again, work in practice to get the feeling of your eyes being set parallel to your target line. Use a mirror at home to make sure your head and eyes are straight; then just bend over and look at an imaginary target line to get the feeling of keeping them parallel.

When you look at your target while addressing the ball, do so by rotating your head, not lifting it. And if you cock your head to the right as you start your swing so you can look at the ball with your left eye, as you

Keep eyes parallel to line of play

Avoid the common mistake of setting your head and eyes askew, especially tilting your head, so your eyeline is pointing to the right of your target line (1). Make sure your head is set straight and your eyes are parallel to your line of play (2). When you look at the target from your address position, rotate your head, keeping the eyeline on a plane parallel to the line of play, instead of lifting your head up and around (3).

should, make sure you rotate it so your chin stays in line with your forehead.

By putting and keeping your eyes in the correct position, that chain reaction of events in your swing can be productive instead of disastrous.

RECAP—SETUP

● Setup incorporates posture—the position of your body parts; aim—the direction in which your clubface is pointing; and alignment—the relationship of your body to your clubface and target line.

● For good posture:
—Stand erect, feet shoulder-width apart, arms hanging at sides.
—Flex knees slightly.
—Bend forward from hips, keeping back straight and sticking out your derriere until arms hang straight down in front of you.
—Repeating the process with a club will determine how far away the ball should be played with each particular club.
—Set your weight toward the balls of your feet, not on the toes or heels. Set it toward the inside of the right foot and evenly on the left, equally distributed between both feet.
—Thrust your knees sideways toward the target and tilt your upper body slightly to the right, placing head behind ball.
—Ideally, your stance should be as narrow as possible with each club, but it should be wide enough to accommodate the force of your swing without restricting leg movement.
—The ball should be positioned two or three inches inside the left heel with all iron shots, slightly forward of that for fairway woods and off your left heel or instep for the driver.

● For good aim:
—In practice, use a line in the turf along your target line or a parallel club or board, then set your clubface square or perpendicular to that line.
—On the course, aim at an intermediate spot a few feet down your intended line of flight instead of the target itself, but always relate your spot to that target.

● For good alignment, set your feet, knees, hips, shoulders and especially your eyes on a line perpendicular to your clubface or parallel to your intended line of play.

FUNDAMENTAL No. 3: USE OF THE LEFT ARM

I think of the golf swing as a circle. The radius of that circle, back and through the shot, is created by the left arm and the club. But we right-handers tend to do most things with the right arm and hand, which are stronger and more skilled than our left. So to be successful in golf, we must switch our thinking from right to left. We must be conscious of, and concentrate on, controlling the swing from start to finish with the left hand and arm.

It isn't easy. The instinct to take over with the right hand is probably stronger than anything else when it comes to the golf swing. It also is probably our most damaging impulse. Even if the rest of your fundamentals are correct, overpowering your left hand and arm with your right will speed up your tempo and ruin your swing. In this chapter I'm going to explain why this is so and help you learn to overcome the problem.

Several years ago I was trying to teach my older brother Ralph something about golf. Ralph is an engineer who hadn't played before, and after I had explained why it is better to control the swing with your left arm rather than your right, he said, "That makes a lot of sense, because a pulling action is much stronger than a pushing action."

He could see immediately that the left or lead arm pulls the club through the forward swing, but if the right began to exert influence, it would have to be a pushing action.

It is also much easier to maintain the radius of the circle, the extension of your swing arc, with the left arm in control. It is not a straight-line action. From a purely mechanical standpoint, the golf swing is a two-lever system, with your left arm the first lever and the club the second lever, your left wrist serving as the hinge.

The left arm swings back, establishing the arc or extension of the swing and sets the club by the cocking of the left hand. On the forward swing, the left arm pulls the club, maintaining its extension and the radius of the arc. This pulling action creates a buildup of centrifugal force that causes the left hand to uncock naturally and releases the club into the ball with the greatest possible speed. Because the left arm can

Left arm is radius of the circle

The simplest way to envision the golf swing is as a circle whose radius is the left arm. With this in mind, it is easy to understand the importance of controlling the swing with the left arm from takeaway through impact and beyond. Any undue influence of the right arm or hand will cause a distortion of your swing circle and a faulty shot.

Keep control in the left arm

While it is important to control your swing with the left arm at all times, it is vital that the left be in control at the top of the swing and the start of the forward swing. This is the critical area in which the right hand and arm are most likely to take over, so concentrate on keeping the left in command at this stage.

continue to accelerate throughout the forward swing, there is nothing to interfere with this buildup of clubhead speed.

The further advantage of left-arm control is the gain in accuracy, in ability to keep the swing on the correct path. Simply stated, you can pull an object straighter than you can push it.

If an outside influence, in this case your right hand and arm, is exerted on the sequence of action I have just described, the system is likely to break down. Once the right starts to take over, either going back or coming forward, it can break down the extension of your arc. It definitely will cause you to "swing from the top," which simply means that your right hand will force the club to release or uncock too soon. This costs you clubhead speed and power. With your right hand and arm in control, your right shoulder is also likely to get into the act and turn too quickly on the forward swing. This forces your arms and the club out of the proper path, causing an inaccurate shot. It also inhibits the action of your legs, further eroding power.

I'm not saying the right side doesn't help in supplying speed and power. You can hit the ball farther with two arms than with just the left alone, so the right is obviously contributing something. But let it con-

On the forward swing, the sequence of movement should be legs (1), arms (2) and clubhead (3). Thinking of keeping the club last in line will promote a proper left-side lead and left-arm control.

tribute as a reaction to the lead of the left. It will happen naturally. Because the right side is so dominant, if we consciously try to use it, it will jump in and overpower the left.

In my clinics I sometimes put so much emphasis on pulling with the left arm that my pupils start to overdo it. They will pull so hard that they will slide their upper bodies sideways to the left. That defeats the whole purpose. So rather than try so hard to pull with the left arm, it might be better for you just to think about the left arm leading the club rather than pulling it. As long as you are simply thinking left arm, your attention is there and not on your right.

A golf professional friend of mine named Tom Scully once wisely told me, "Keep the club last in line." As long as you keep the club last in line on the forward swing, your left arm will be leading it rather than your right arm pushing it.

The more you are able to keep your left arm in control of the swing, the better your tempo will be. Because the right-side takeover is instinctive and therefore fast, it will speed up everything. Just *thinking* about the left arm will slow down your swing and help keep it under control so the speed and power can be applied at the right time.

Swing left arm straight back and up

On the backswing, your sensation should be that your left arm is swinging straight back away from the ball and straight up. The natural turning of your upper body will move the club inside your line of play and into correct position at the top.

Correct use of the left arm begins when you set up to the ball. At that point you should be holding the club lightly with the left hand and arm. The right hand should only be resting on the club, the right arm hanging relaxed and bent. If the right arm is straight or tense, it will be in a dominant position to start with and will want to take over the swing immediately. If that happens, it's going to control the swing all the way.

I feel that I swing the left hand, left arm and left shoulder back as a unit. If I really analyze what I do, I suppose the left arm is leading the way and causing the shoulder to turn, but I feel that everything happens together.

With the right arm very relaxed, the left arm swings back straight away from the ball and up. It doesn't go straight up, of course. It swings to the inside of your starting path and back up approximately over your right shoulder. That's where your posture at address has such an influence. If your upper-body tilt is correct and your arms are hanging naturally, your arms will swing back to the top, turning to the inside and rotating naturally into the correct position. Your sensation should just be to swing your left arm straight back away from the ball and then straight up.

During the backswing, keep the left arm as straight and relaxed as possible. It should not be locked or rigid, because that obviously will

tighten up your swing, costing you fluidity and speed. But you should work on keeping the arm straight, because that gives you the maximum extension. Also, once the left arm bends and starts to break down, the easier it is for the right hand to take over.

Try to swing your hands as high as you can on the backswing, because that gives you the biggest possible arc. It keeps you very firm at the top and prepares you to start back down. But be sure the left hand and arm remain in control of the swing.

I see a lot of golfers trying to get the club parallel to the ground or past parallel at the top of the swing, thinking that will give them a longer swing and more power. Mostly, I see them doing that by breaking down their hands or the left arm, and almost always they do it with the right hand or shoulder. That extra length does more harm than good because it breaks down the lever system and puts the right side in control.

Actually, the key to an *effective* big arc is getting the hands high and keeping the left hand firm and in control at the top, with no looseness or flippiness. Getting flippy at the top is the quickest way to get fast, which ruins your tempo and gets your right side into play. My club rarely gets to parallel, even with the driver, because that left hand and wrist are firm up there, but my arc is plenty big because my hands are high.

When you are in correct position at the top, your left arm will have

Swing down underneath your chin

From the top, the left arm simply swings down in a circle underneath your chin. If you begin your forward swing properly with your lower body, your arms and club will be routed into the ball on the correct path.

rotated so that your left thumb is underneath the shaft and supporting it. You should feel a definite tautness in your left arm and shoulder and across the left upper portion of your back. All the right hand and arm are doing is providing some support for the club at the top. If you feel any tension in the right side, it means the right side is about to take over.

Once you start down from the top, you should feel that the left arm is simply going to swing underneath your chin. Again, that gets right back to the concept of having your arms hang naturally at address. When you swing them back, they are going to want to return to that position naturally. So my feeling is—and yours should be—that the left arm is simply making a circle underneath my chin on the forward swing. It returns on the same path on which it went back. I look at somebody like Gene Littler, and it all seems so simple—he just turns and returns. It probably feels that simple to him too.

Many good players and teachers contend that the arms and the club swing down on a path inside of that on which they swung back, and that's probably true. I'm sure it's to be desired—certainly much more than swinging down *outside* your backswing path. But I've never been able to consciously re-route the club on the forward swing, and I don't think most amateur players can either.

I do believe, however, that correct leg action on the forward swing

will drop the club to a more inside path. We'll get into that in the next chapter. So I feel that when you are working with your left arm, it's sufficient just to think of swinging it forward on the same path it took going back.

The good player controls his swing all the way to the finish with his left arm. But once you have started forward, there is not much you can do to change your swing, because there isn't enough time. So you will have to preprogram into your swing what you want to happen.

For example, I prefer to fade the ball, aiming down the left side and letting the ball drift back into the center. I do this by "holding on" a little longer with my left arm. In other words, I don't let it rotate counter-clockwise or to the left quite as quickly as it might normally want to. That keeps the clubface square or slightly open as it comes through impact.

If I want to hook the ball—and that's difficult for me to do—I'll try to release or rotate more quickly with the left arm, turning it over and closing the clubface a bit.

When you first start working with the left arm, I'd recommend that you let it rotate naturally. Just think of swinging it underneath you and out toward the target. You will find, I think, that the left hand will release or uncock naturally and at the right time, provided you don't do anything to interfere with it. Once you become more proficient, you can get cute and

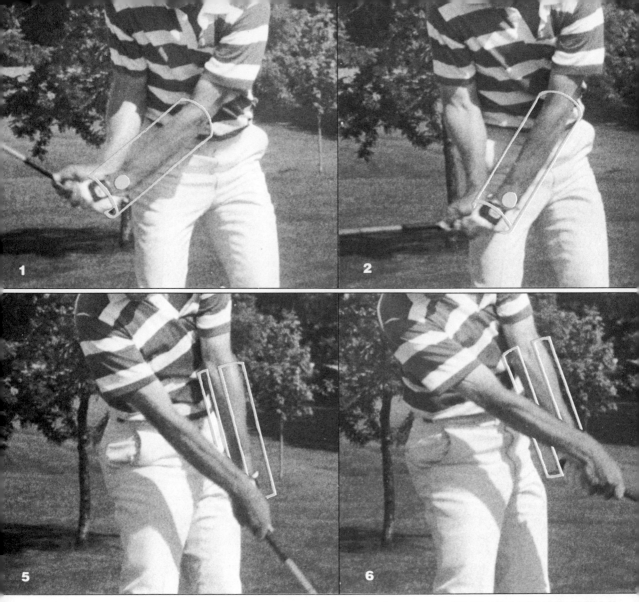

Left arm, hand rotate as a unit

The "release" of your hands and club is accomplished by a rotation of your left forearm and hand as a unit. The left hand uncocks at the wrist as the forearm rotates, but the back of the left hand remains in the same relationship to the left arm throughout the swing. Even as the right hand and arm cross over the left through impact, there is no hinging or flapping at the left wrist.

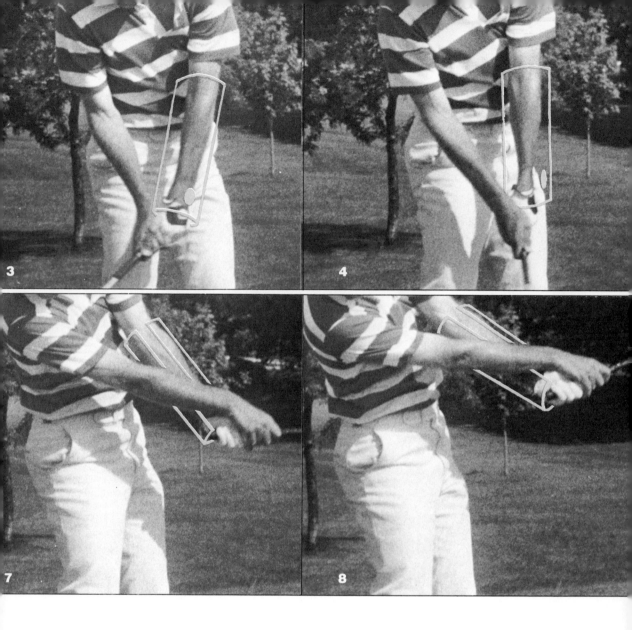

Finish with your hands high

Before you swing, program yourself to finish with your hands high. This will improve your acceleration through the shot.

try to manipulate the ball with your left arm.

Keep in mind that when I talk about "rotation" and "release," I mean a rotation of the left forearm and the left hand while the left wrist remains firm. The back of the left hand remains in the same relationship to the left arm throughout the swing that it started in at address. There should be no flapping or breaking down at the wrist as you swing through impact. As the forearm rotates and your body turns, the right arm and hand naturally cross over the left as you swing into your follow-through.

As I said, once you start forward with your swing, there is nothing you can do with it. But I find it helpful to think beforehand about finishing high with my hands. It seems to improve my acceleration through the shot and should do the same for you.

Since the left arm is so important in the golf swing, and since it is inherently weaker than the right, it is a good idea to do some exercises that will strengthen it. I still do them myself. Squeeze a rubber ball or other grip-strengthening device while you are in your car or watching television. Choke down on a club and, using just your left hand and keeping your wrist firm, raise it and lower it to develop the forearm muscles. Or point the club straight up in the air with your arm extended straight in front of you and rotate the club from 9 o'clock to 3 o'clock.

Swing a club with just your left hand. Hit balls with just your left hand. Not only does that strengthen your left side, it also shows you that because your left arm is weaker you need to swing more slowly and develop good tempo and timing to have a controlled swing.

Sometimes I play tennis left-handed. That helps develop my left arm, and it also shows me how playing golf has helped me strengthen my left side. I have a pretty good natural left-handed backhand on the tennis court, thanks to making the same motion all these years on the golf course.

In doing any of these exercises or activities, of course, take care not to overdo things and hurt yourself. But do them. It will pay off in a stronger left side and a better swing.

RECAP—USE OF THE LEFT ARM

With the club hanging in control of the left hand at address, swing the left arm straight back and up.

Keep the left arm as straight as possible without being locked or rigid.

Swing the left hand as high as possible without letting the right take over.

Keep the left hand firm at the top—the left thumb should be underneath the shaft and the back of the left hand should be in the same relationship to the left arm as it was at address.

Swing the left arm forward on the same route on which you took it back.

Feel that you are swinging in a circle underneath you and out toward the target.

Allow the arm to rotate and the hand to release or uncock naturally as you swing through to a high finish.

FUNDAMENTAL No. 4: USE OF THE LEGS

How the legs work in the golf swing is a mystery to many amateurs, maybe most amateurs, probably because they are trying to make it too difficult. They are not able to relate leg action in the golf swing to other common activities.

I was on a local television show some time ago with a tennis professional. We were discussing the common traits and the common faults of the two sports. At one point there was a split-screen image showing me hitting a golf shot and him hitting a tennis shot, and it was uncanny how much alike the action was in the two shots.

Virtually anytime you hit something or throw something, the basic body actions are the same. A baseball swing is the same as a golf swing, except it's on a different plane. Toss a ball to someone a few yards away and notice how your legs work instinctively as your weight goes from the right leg to the left. And the farther you want to throw the ball, the more your legs are going to work. If you rear back to throw an overhand fastball, you're going to make a big stride. Yet the action of the legs remains basically the same. It's just magnified.

The resemblance is to a pulling action, the leg movement preceding the swinging of the arms and finally the release of the ball. You can even see the same kind of action in a basketball player shooting a free throw. He crouches, bends the knees, then straightens them as he straightens his upper body, extends his arm and finally releases the ball. The leg movement precedes everything.

You don't reverse the procedure. You don't shoot a free throw with stiff legs. You don't throw or hit a ball without moving your legs. You'll move them instinctively, because if you don't you might fall down.

And that's exactly the function the legs perform in a golf swing. *Your legs move to allow the body to turn and the arms to swing.* While a certain amount of power can be added to the swing by good leg action, you must realize, at the beginning, that the main thing the legs do is provide support for the movement of the upper body. Very simply, on the backswing, the left leg is pulled around by the swinging of the arms and

Throwing or hitting, legs work the same

To illustrate to yourself the basic leg action in golf, toss a ball underhand to a target a few yards away. Notice how the legs move prior to the forward swing of the arm. Your legs will end up in a position remarkably similar to that at the finish of a soft pitch shot.

the turning of the body. On the forward swing, the legs move first so they can provide a foundation for the arm swing and body turn.

You don't see any good players on tour who don't have good leg action, sometimes a lot of leg action. You hear players talk about leg drive and generating power with the legs, and it does seem as if a lot of the better players and bigger hitters are men with bigger, stronger legs.

But that can be misleading, and using the legs to generate power can be overdone. The players with stronger legs generally have stronger arms and upper bodies too. It's quite likely that they are making a stronger leg drive simply to accommodate a stronger and faster swinging of the arms.

Frankly, I wouldn't attempt to use your legs for power unless you are an advanced player. If you use your legs properly, you will get more power without trying, because you will be allowing a bigger turn and a bigger arc. Your tempo also will be better. If you don't use your legs correctly, you will cut off your sources of power. Also, if your legs don't work, you instinctively will overwork your hands to compensate. As I'll explain later, that's the last thing you want to have happen.

Once you have acquired a feel for the proper leg action and can time it with the swinging of your arms and turning of your upper body,

then you can experiment with faster, stronger leg movement to see what it does for you in the way of increased distance.

Correct use of the legs begins with correct posture, because that puts the legs in position to move properly. If your posture is bad, it is difficult for you to use your legs. Lack of leg action then breeds excessive hand action and other compensations that throw your tempo and your swing out of whack.

Stance width, which is a part of posture, has a lot to do with how well you use your legs. If your stance is too wide, it will lock the legs and prevent them from moving well beneath you. If your stance is too narrow, your leg action will be naturally inhibited by a fear of losing your balance.

So pay attention to the posture guidelines I discussed in Chapter 4 and you will be off to a good start in learning to use your legs properly.

Let me say something here about your feet—*bring them to life*. A lot of people try to play golf with their feet nailed to the ground, and that rarely works. The feet have a dynamic role to play. Unless you are extraordinarily supple, the left heel comes off the ground on the backswing and the right heel comes up on the forward swing.

Some good teachers and players advocate consciously moving the feet instead of the legs on the theory that if the feet move, the legs

have to move also. I don't know that I would entirely agree with that, mainly because I believe the movement of the legs on the backswing is a reaction to the turning of the body. But if you are having trouble getting your feet unglued from the ground, consciously thinking of working with them during practice can be a good way to loosen them and get them to act in concert with the correct, fluid leg action.

Let's take a detailed look at how the legs work during the swing. But as we do, please bear in mind that while I'm going to be describing *position*, what the legs do, I want you to be thinking about how the leg action *feels*. Most of the positions I will be describing are reactions to other actions or thoughts. The movement of the legs through these positions results in a total feel that you must identify before you can successfully incorporate the proper use of your legs into your swing.

Legs allow the body to turn

Going back, the left side is swung around a firm but flexed right leg, which rotates just slightly as the hips turn (1). The left knee is pulled freely toward the right and the left heel is pulled off the ground. Coming forward, the legs move laterally and in a rotary fashion, your balance point going to the left foot and right toe through impact (2). The turning of the hips and legs must be greater on the follow-through (3) to allow the turning of your upper body through the shot.

On the backswing, the leg action is particularly uncomplicated because you don't have to think about it. It happens as a reaction to the swinging of your left arm and the turning of your upper body. As the upper body turns, the hips are pulled around. This in turn causes the left knee to rotate outward and back toward the right. Finally, the left heel is pulled off the ground— the bigger the swing, the more it comes up. Allowing the left heel to come up naturally lets you make a longer backswing. This helps your tempo, because your swing doesn't feel so rushed.

While this is happening, the right leg remains flexed but firm, as stationary as possible. There is a slight rotation of the upper right leg as the hips turn, but this is limited. You are trying to keep your weight on the inside of your right foot, or at the very least flat on your foot. Never let the

First move down—
replant left heel

Allow the left heel to be pulled off the ground on the backswing, and to start the forward swing replant the left heel exactly where it was at address. This gets the lower body started first and induces the correct sequence of movement on the forward swing.

weight go to the outside of the right foot.

When I am swinging well, I have the feeling that I am turning my left side around my right side, with the right leg acting as a pivot. The legs are fairly passive on the backswing, there being only as much movement as the upper body dictates. That's why I hasten to correct the golfers—and there are many—who ask me where the left knee should be pointed on the backswing. It shouldn't consciously be pointed anywhere, because any such movement will break down your extension, create too much lower-body movement and throw your swing out of sync.

Just as you turned your body *away* from the target going back, on the forward swing you want to turn your body all the way *toward* the target. Your legs must move to allow that turn, and they must move first. If your hands, arms or shoulders move first on the forward swing, your

Legs lead change of direction

At the top of your swing, or during the club's change of direction, the legs make the initial move forward. This often happens while the arms and club are still swinging back, although it is not so pronounced in Geiberger's swing. The early movement of the legs supports the swinging of the arms and club coming forward.

Finish on the left foot, right toe

At the finish of your swing, your weight should be balanced on the outside edge of your left foot, toward the heel, and on your right toe, with your stomach pointing approximately to your target.

upper body will tend to slide toward the target and your legs will go dead as a reaction. Then they won't be able to support the swinging of the arms and the turning of the body.

The thought that triggers my forward swing is to replant my left heel exactly where it was at address, at the same time keeping my upper body where it was at the top of the swing, behind the ball. Replanting that left heel gets everything started correctly. It gets the legs moving, which allows your upper body to stay behind the ball, where it belongs, as you swing through impact.

Once the left heel is replanted, the left knee moves laterally a few inches and turns in a rotary motion. The right knee thrusts more directly toward the target, although it too turns as the upper body turns.

That's what happens. What you *feel* happening may vary with the individual. Although there is no doubt in my mind that the left leg is leading the forward swing, I personally feel a thrusting of my right hip and right knee toward the target. I also feel a bit of sliding action with my hips, but this sensation comes more from the bowing of my body as my hips turn rather than slide.

Still, I believe that if you simply think of replanting the left heel while keeping your upper body in place, your legs are going to work just fine. Whatever sliding and turning actions take place are going to happen naturally if you follow these two guidelines.

I don't consciously think about replanting the left heel because it's a natural reaction for me. But you probably will have to think about it and work on doing it in practice for a while. Practice the movement without a ball in front of you. Then practice it while striking balls on the range. It won't be long before the movement will become instinctive for you too, and your legs will be doing what they are supposed to do.

To determine if your legs are working correctly, check your finish position. Your left foot should have rolled onto its outside edge, with the weight on the outside and toward the heel. You should be up on your right toe, your upper body and hips turned so your belt buckle is facing approximately to your target. If you aren't in this position, your legs haven't played their role correctly. That usually means you haven't allowed them to work properly because you made a wrong move at the wrong time somewhere else.

I'll expand on that next when we put the swing together.

RECAP—USE OF THE LEGS

● The legs move to allow the body to turn and the arms to swing in both directions. If the legs don't move properly, the hands will take over.

● On the backswing, the left leg turns around a firm but flexed right leg as a reaction to the swinging of the left arm and the turning of the body. The left heel is pulled off the ground.

● To start the forward swing, replant the left heel.

● The left knee then moves laterally and around, turning the left hip, left shoulder and left arm in a chain reaction.

● If your hands, arms, or shoulders move first on the forward swing, your legs will go dead and won't be able to support the swinging of the arms and turning of the body.

● If your legs work correctly, at the finish you should be balanced on the outside of your left foot and on your right toe, your belt buckle facing approximately to the target.

FINDING YOUR OWN BEST TEMPO

Now that you are familiar with my four fundamental areas, the *parts* of the swing and how they work, we must put them together into a *complete* swing, one in which those parts interact at the right pace and in the correct sequence. This blending of parts into a whole gives you the tempo and the timing you need to strike the ball well.

In this chapter I will give you—and in some cases repeat—a few thoughts that will put the overall swing in clearer perspective for you; I will take you through the swing slowly to make certain you know how everything works together in proper sequence, and I will finish with some thoughts that will enhance your tempo and make your swing more effective.

In its simplest form, what is a golf swing? What is your body doing? Your body is simply making *a turn and a return*. All you do is make the moves that allow you to do that.

I've mentioned the importance of having your head behind or to the right of the ball at address. This is because at address you want to come as close as you can to your impact position. If you achieve this at address, all you have to do is turn back and return to that position. You won't look quite the same at impact, of course, because your legs are moving quite rapidly at that point. But the *thought* of just returning to your address position can simplify your swing image.

To do this you must *keep* your head in the same relative position it was in at address. That's so your legs and hips can lead the swing and create the left-side pulling action you need. Once your head and upper body start sliding toward the target, they get ahead of your legs and your legs go dead. There is no way you can continue a nice turn through the ball, so your hands instinctively take over to provide clubhead speed. In most cases, that will not get the job done.

The swing is a circle, and on the forward swing the club is being pulled around that circle with the left arm. For all practical purposes, your head is the hub around which that circle revolves. Anytime you move that hub in the same direction as you are swinging, you will break

down your left-side extension and lose clubhead speed.

Don't try to keep your head rigid. It can rotate and even move a little. Your thought should be that everything is swinging around your head— your upper body is turning and winding around your head going back, and your legs are working underneath your head coming forward. This causes a good forward movement onto the left side and creates the left-arm action that leads the club through the shot.

As I've said, my thought is to keep my head and upper body in one place as I swing forward. It's similar to the old "swing in a barrel" philosophy. I feel I just "stay there" with my upper body and when I do that, it's amazing how well my legs work down below.

I haven't said much about hands so far, except negatively. And you

3

Turn and return

The golf swing is really only a turn and a return—from your address position, the upper body responds to the swinging of the arms by turning or winding approximately 90 degrees. On the forward swing, it returns or unwinds to approximately the address position at impact, then keeps turning through the finish of the swing.

won't catch me saying much positive about hands, because I believe an emphasis on the hands to be one of the great destroyers of the swing. That's why it is so important to use your legs and swing your left arm correctly. For every action there's an equal and opposite reaction, and if your legs and arms aren't working, your hands will, usually detrimentally.

Your hands must be set on the club properly, because that allows the club to react correctly to the swinging of the left arm. That's essentially what hand action is in the golf swing—a reaction to the working of the legs and the swinging of the arms. The firmer you can keep your hands and wrist action—notice I didn't say tight or rigid—during the swing, the better off you will be.

Keep head behind the ball throughout the swing

These comparative sequences show how the head and upper body remain behind the ball at address and throughout the swing. Note that with a 5-iron (top sequence), Geiberger's head is set just slightly behind the ball, because this allows the correct descending swing into the ball. With the driver (bottom), the head and upper body are set farther behind the ball to promote the level or ascending swing that is needed when the ball is on a tee.

1   2   3   4

Hands remain 'quiet'

This sequence shows that there is no conscious use of the hands during the swing. Note how quiet the hands remain as the arms swing down from the top. From picture 1 to 3 the hands actually cock more, indicating the pulling action of the arms and the absence of any independent hand action. As the arms swing into the impact area, the centrifugal force built up in the clubhead causes the hands to uncock naturally and bring the clubface squarely into the ball.

Tommy Bolt was one of the best examples of that. He seemed not to use his hands at all in his swing, emphasizing good leg action, body turn and arm swing. And he was one of the greatest strikers of the ball we've ever had.

I make a lot of practice swings with no hand action at all to make sure my legs and arms are working correctly. One of the most common faults I see in amateurs is an overuse of the hands, too much setting or cocking on the backswing and a too-early release coming forward. I tell them to feel as if they are swinging with no wrist break at all. Usually they end up with about the right amount.

The hands *do* work, of course. Unless you make a conscious effort to keep them rigid and immobile, the hands will cock going back, as a result of the swinging action of the club. Coming forward, they will uncock just as naturally, as a result of the centrifugal force created by the buildup of clubhead speed. The effective weight of your club is so great as you near the bottom of your swing that your hands have to uncock. But if you are thinking of swinging your left arm instead of using those hands, they will uncock at the right time, bringing the clubhead

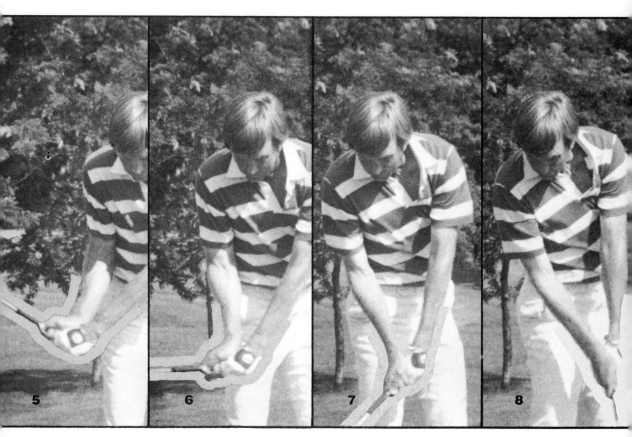

squarely into the ball.

A further advantage to keeping the hands out of the swing is that you increase your effective hitting area. Players with a lot of hand action, which is the way almost everyone played in the pre-modern era, turn the club over quickly through the impact area, which means it doesn't stay square to the target line for more than an instant. On the other hand, the good modern player who uses more leg action and lets the swinging of his arms square the club naturally can keep the face on target a lot longer. That leads to much more consistency.

The best analogy I can give you for a picture of correct hand action may be striking a nail with a hammer. When you do that, you don't keep your wrist and arm stiff. There is a bit of natural setting or cocking going up. Coming down, you don't flick the hammerhead at the nail with your hand. If you did, you would hit your thumb. You swing the hammer down into the nail with your arm, letting the weight of the hammer itself uncock your hand and bring the head squarely onto the head of the nail.

That's the way the hands should work in the golf swing too, if you will just let it happen.

At 6–2, I'm considered a tall player, and I'm often asked if there are special techniques that a player of my height must use. My answer is, "Basically, no." The same fundamentals apply to golfers of all sizes and shapes. The advice I just gave, to keep the hands firm during the swing, applies particularly to the tall golfer. The only other emphasis I would make is that the taller player pay particular attention to achieving correct posture, and he should take advantage of his height by making sure he gets the maximum arc out of his swing. Being tall can be an advantage if you don't become self-conscious and cramp your swing. A full, free pass at the ball will pay off in more distance and potentially lower scores.

Through the Swing Slowly

Let me take you through the swing, describing the sequence in which things happen and what you should feel as they happen.

The club is started back with the left hand, left arm and left shoulder moving in unison, swinging the clubhead straight back and up. Make no independent manipulation with your hands. You are controlling the club with the last three fingers of your left hand, and because you are doing this your hands will begin to cock naturally as you swing back past waist-high.

As your arms swing and your shoulders turn, your left leg is being pulled back and around, and your left heel is lifted off the ground. Your right leg remains firm but flexed, your weight never going to the outside of your right foot.

Swing the club back as far as you can with your left arm and shoulder, but don't try to get it back any farther by grabbing with the right hand or forcing the right shoulder farther back. At the top of the swing your left hand should feel firm and in control of the club.

To start the forward swing, replant the left heel in the same position it was in at address. Then, with no feeling of anxiety or hurry, swing the left arm straight down on the path on which it came back, keeping your head and upper body in place behind the ball while your legs work underneath you.

As you start the forward swing, your hands remain cocked. They will uncock naturally, without your thinking about it, as your arms swing through the shot.

During the forward swing I have the sensation that my right side is working *underneath* my left, pushing out on the left side and producing the bowing action of the body. I feel my legs working and the pulling action of my left arm, which is always in control. But I do feel that my right side, although relaxed, is pretty active.

At the same time, the left side is feeling stretched and extended. Once you lose that feeling, you have broken down somewhere and immediately will lose power and direction in your swing.

With the left side stretched, the left arm pulling and the right side coming naturally into play, your primary sensation becomes swinging your arms and the club *through* the ball and out down the target line. If you do that, your hands will finish high, your belt buckle (or the equivalent) will wind up facing the target, and your weight will be properly distributed on the outside of your left foot and your right toe.

A good drill to help you finish your swing is to make sure you hang onto the club with your hands all the way through to the end. Don't let your fingers, especially on the left hand, slip off the club. Just hang on and let your body be pulled around into the correct finish position.

While all of my four fundamentals are vital in producing that good tempo, I think the two most important are using the legs properly and controlling the swing with your left arm. The two are strongly linked.

Controlling with the left arm from start to finish maintains the unity, the completeness of your swing. It prevents the breakdowns that cause your swing to speed up, the most common being the takeover by the right hand at the top. When you grab with the right hand, it is going to move faster and cause everything else to do the same.

Your left arm can move only so fast. If you are right-handed, it can't move as fast as your right hand and arm because it isn't as strong. Therefore, a conscious effort to control the swing with your left arm will automatically slow it down. And the correct use of your legs on the forward swing gives you a much better chance of maintaining control with that left arm.

I know that when I want to make a hard swing, I make sure that I remain firm with the left hand and arm. If that breaks down, my tempo and timing are destroyed.

The same thought will work for you. If nothing is moving faster than the force that is controlling your swing—your left arm—your tempo and timing will fall nicely into place.

Make Your Swing Arc As Long As You Can

Because of my "keep it simple" theory, I used to have a short swing, especially for a tall guy. I just figured that if I kept my swing as short as possible, there was less that could go wrong with it. But I was mistaken, as I've since discovered. The shorter the swing, the harder it is to have good tempo and timing, because everything is condensed into such a short period of time.

I look admiringly at a player like Doug Sanders, who seemed like he could swing in the proverbial telephone booth. It looked as if his hands never got past shoulder-high on his backswing. What a tremendous talent, what great timing and feel he must have had to play as well as he did! Doug won 20 tournaments between 1956 and 1972, and for a period of years was one of the very best players on our tour.

Make your swing long

The longer your swing, the better chance you have for things to happen in the proper sequence and the more clubhead speed you can build through impact. Think of swinging your hands high and finishing your backswing, without making any movements that disrupt the arc of your swing, to make that arc as long as possible.

It may be more than coincidence, however, that while Doug's career lasted less than 20 years, Sam Snead has kept his long, flowing swing working at near-perfection for more than 45. Homero Blancas, who played successfully on tour for about 10 years, once said to me, "I know I don't have as many years out here as a lot of people because my swing is so short."

I came to a similar conclusion, which is why my swing is now a lot longer than it used to be. In the first place, it's easier to have good tempo—and consequently good timing—with a longer swing, because there is more time for things to happen and you don't feel as rushed. With a Snead-type swing, you're in no hurry. You swing back to the top and it seems as if you have all day to get collected and start back down. You know your arc is big enough to give you all the clubhead speed you need.

If your swing is short, everything is a little more critical—the timing is more sensitive, a little more effort must be put into the swing and there is more wear-and-tear on the nerves. You instinctively feel the need to hit the ball harder because your swing is shorter, whereas in a long swing everything seems easier and more natural.

The length of your swing, of course, will be limited by your physical characteristics—your build and your flexibility. But those should be the only limitations. Within the guidelines I have given you, you should attempt to make your swing as long as possible.

Finish Your Backswing

Jack Nicklaus has said that when he faces a critical shot, the one thought he has is to finish his backswing. That's a good thought for everybody on every shot. I know that when I take what is a full swing for me and complete the backswing, it's a beautiful sensation. I feel as if I'm in complete control of my swing, in perfect position with all my power ready to be used—I think of it as being "collected" up there. Suddenly there's this great feeling that you have all day to get back down. There's no rush to hit the ball. You have coiled the spring and it uncoils almost without your having to think about it.

Mike Souchak was still playing a lot when I first started on tour, and I was a great admirer of his swing. He always looked as if he had the club in perfect position at the top and then everything uncoiled together. That's the feeling I have—everything starts down as a unit. Technically that may not be true, because my legs probably initiate the forward swing, but my feeling is that everything goes together.

A caution here—while I emphasize that you finish your backswing and maybe even feel a slight pause at the top, I don't advocate that you *stop* up there: It's a very fine line, I know, but when you stop it's difficult to get started again. You lose the fluidity in your swing. You've turned what should be one smooth swing into two separate movements. You see good players—Cary Middlecoff, Dan Sikes and Bob Murphy, for example—who seem to stop at the top. I'm not sure they really do. Their lower bodies probably are starting the forward swing while the club appears to be fixed at the top. But even if they do stop, bear in mind that these players have a lot more talent than the average amateur and can get away with it.

Start Down as You Went Up

When you start down from the top, it's important to do it at the same pace you went up. Just as I like to feel leisurely when I'm swinging the club back, so I like to feel leisurely starting it down. It's as if you are *letting* your body uncoil and your arms swing the club down, without forcing.

It doesn't always happen that way, of course. There are times when I don't get "collected" at the top, when I feel myself starting down before I get up there. My tendency is to get a little quick at the top and slide

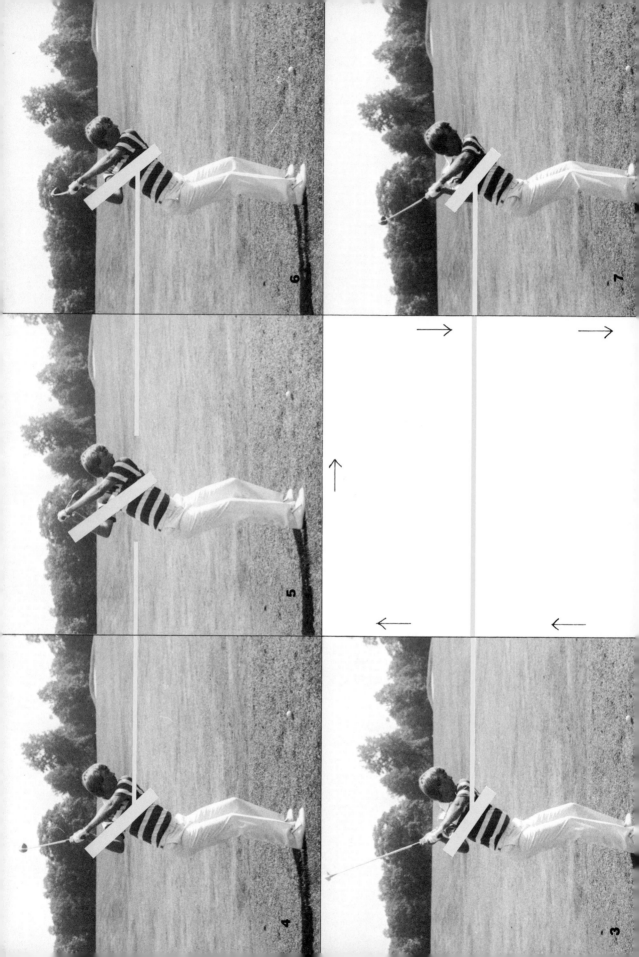

Start down as you went up

To best maintain your tempo through the forward swing, feel as if you are starting down as you went up—at the same pace and in basically the same positions. Without forcing, allow your arms to swing down in a leisurely manner, following the same path they took on the backswing.

Think of the clubhead

Thinking of the clubhead, trying to feel it and know where it is throughout your swing, will take your mind off mechanics and will slow down the pace of your swing.

forward a little bit with my left shoulder. Then I'm out of position all the way down and get a mediocre shot at best.

Usually I know what causes that. I was in a poor position at address. I like to aim a little left of my target and fade the ball, and sometimes I creep too far left. Then my left shoulder has too far to go to make a full turn and suddenly I've come up with a short swing.

That gets back to my point that improper fundamentals can cause poor tempo. If you have a bad grip or bad posture or bad alignment, or you are not using the parts of your body correctly during the swing, you'll have trouble getting into that correct position at the top. You can't get collected, so you can never get that sensation of starting everything down together in a leisurely fashion. You instinctively know you are out of position and must make some manipulation to get the club back on track. This creates the anxiety that causes you to get too fast and destroy your tempo.

When I'm hitting the ball well, I feel as if I just go up and start down

92

exactly the same way—just up and return and the ball is on its way. Everything falls into place.

Think Feel, Not Technique

I was working with my son John one day and couldn't get him to slow down his backswing. Then I remembered something my pro, Jim Blakeley, had told me when I was a youngster—*just think of the clubhead, feel the clubhead, throughout the swing*. When you do that it's amazing how your swing slows down. If you know where the clubhead is during the swing, it somehow makes it easier to keep a good pace and build up for that one big moment through the ball.

Thinking of the clubhead also takes your mind off technique, and that's the main point I'm trying to make. In the learning stages, paying attention to the mechanics of the game is crucial. But you can get so involved with technique, with so many thoughts running through your mind, that you forget your primary purpose is to swing the clubhead through the ball and get the ball to your target. Once your mind gets confused, it's very easy to get too fast. You crank the club away too quickly at the start; you forget about the clubhead and you can never find it again during the swing. Chances are you won't get it very solidly on the ball either.

One of my good friends on tour was Jay Hebert, the 1960 PGA champion. Jay was very technique-conscious. I've always felt that he analyzed the swing so much that he almost lost sight of tempo. He was a great player, but I think he could have been even better had he concentrated more on tempo instead of technique.

There are certain things you can think about before you swing. In fact, you *must* think about grip, stance, posture, alignment and all the preparatory fundamentals. But when you are ready to make the swing, one positive thought is enough. When I realized I was teaching my son so much technique that we were overlooking the basic swing concept, I gave him Blakeley's thought—feel the clubhead. Right away his back-swing slowed.

There are other thoughts or sensations you can develop that will help your tempo. For example, Sam Snead says he likes his swing to feel "oily." That's an excellent thought, because he's really ingraining a fluid sensation in his mind. Anytime you are thinking of a fluid swing, you will instinctively swing more slowly and easily in the early stages.

After all, *feel* is the overriding factor in good tempo. You *think* about the correct pace to your swing, concentrating on some thought that works for you, but that thought must be transferred into a *feel* in your muscles before it will work.

Here is a quick and simple review of the fundamentals that have been covered in the last five chapters:

1. Your grip tells the clubface where to go. Your hands should be positioned on the club as closely as possible to the way they hang naturally at your side, keeping in mind that you want your palms facing as much as possible in a "neutral" position. This allows your arms to swing freely and rotate, the clubface squaring itself without any manipulation from the hands.

2. Your setup involves the posture of your body, the aiming of your clubface and the alignment of your body with the clubface. First, aim your clubface down your target line, then align your feet, knees, hips, shoulders and eyes parallel to that line. Your knees should be flexed slightly, and you should be bent forward from the hips enough that your arms hang naturally and can swing freely.

3. The left arm controls the swing. With a light but firm pressure in the last three fingers of the left hand, the left arm swings the club back and pulls it through on a circle. The right side will complement the swing, but the right hand and arm never should be allowed to take over.

4. The legs move to allow the body to make a complete turn and the arms to swing. On the backswing, the left leg is pulled around and back by the turning of the upper body around a firm but flexed right leg. On the forward swing, the left heel is replanted and the legs lead the way to provide support for the arm swing and body turn.

5. Timing is putting the parts of the swing together in the proper sequence. In its simplest form, the swing is a turn and a return to an impact position with the club that is as close to your address position as you can get it. The left arm swings back and the upper body turns, the left leg following. The legs lead coming forward, turning the left side and helping the left arm pull the club. Your head and upper body remain in place behind the ball as you swing the club through the ball and out toward the target. Your swing should be as long and as unhurried as possible. Your left arm should always be in control because this allows you to swing at a pace that insures good timing.

Work with the four fundamentals in practice, individually and in concert as you put them together with the correct timing. The longer you practice them, the more natural it will become for you to perform the actions correctly. When you get on the course, you can't be thinking about that many things, and soon you won't have to. I'm sure you will end up with a key thought or two that will work to trigger your swing. Stick with that thought and don't clutter your mind with any other details while you are playing.

But be sure you keep returning to your fundamentals in practice. Like a fine car or any machine, the golf swing needs constant tuning to keep it in good working order. It can slip out of adjustment quite easily, and when it does you must go back to your fundamentals to get it fixed.

The next three chapters will be devoted to the short game and to finesse shots. The fundamentals I have given you for the full swing apply as well to the rest of the game. From the putt to the drive, the golf swing should be essentially the same, with only minor variations in grip and stance to fit the situation. It makes the game a lot simpler.

TEMPO AROUND THE GREEN

I don't think I'll get much argument when I tell you that the short game is the most important area of golf. The ability to successfully execute these little shots on and around the green distinguishes the tour professional from the amateur and, at any level, the winner from the loser.

No matter how skilled a player you may be, you seldom will hit every green during a round. Even if you do, you still have to putt the ball in the hole. So shooting a good score always boils down to your ability to execute the little recovery shots and/or the putts.

That's why all you have learned so far in this book becomes so important as we move into this area. As vital as good tempo is in the full swing, it is probably even more so in the short-game shots. These shots depend so much on touch and feel that any excessive quickening of your swing will create havoc. Fortunately, if you have paid attention in the preceding chapters, you are well-prepared to overcome any tempo-ruining tendencies, even if you have had trouble with the short shots in the past.

Most amateur golfers I see make the short shots much too difficult. They seem to think there is something different and mysterious about them. In reality, all you do with any of these shots, including the putt, is *capture a certain moment of the swing*.

Each of the short shots is simply a miniature swing. There are some variations, mainly having to do with your setup for each particular shot, but the fundamentals of the full swing apply as well to the less-than-full swing. Just as in the full swing, if you apply these fundamentals, you can achieve the tempo you need for success in the mini-swings.

Assuming you set up to the ball free of tension, proper application of the fundamentals will let you swing without tension. This absence of tension allows a good tempo and gives you a better chance to strike the ball at the right moment and with the right amount of acceleration.

The key fundamental on all short shots except the putt is proper use of the legs. It also may be the most overlooked fundamental, both by teachers and players. Most amateurs simply do not use their legs in

NO

YES

Keep left hand firm through impact

For effective chipping, there must be no breakdown or cupping of the left hand (left). The left hand and arm should remain in a firm, straight-line relationship (right) through impact and beyond.

chipping, pitching and sand play. They stand stiff-legged and instead of using the bigger, more relaxed muscles, they rely on their hands. This results in a wristy swing, and it's hard to build any kind of consistency that way.

In the sections that follow, I'll relate the application of this, the other fundamentals and the resulting good tempo to each of the short shots and tell you how you can start reducing your scores by developing skill in this vital area.

Chipping

A chip is any shot in which you are trying to get the ball down on the green quickly and let it run as far as possible on its way to the hole. Because it is a running shot, just one step away from a putt, it is made with a firm-wristed stroke. Simply swing the left arm back and through with the hands leading the clubhead.

Because the chipping stroke is so short, you must make a compensation in setting up to the ball if the stroke is to work as it should. Ideally, at impact in a full swing your knees thrust toward the target as your lower body turns and your weight shifts to the left. Left hand, arm and side lead the club through the ball. But you don't have time in such a compact stroke for all this to happen, unless you help yourself by the way you set up. The key is to *assume the impact position at address*.

Your posture basics remain the same. Bend from the hips so your arms hang naturally. Your knees should be flexed. Choke down on the club. This gives you better control for the more delicate shot you are about to make. The longer the chip, the less you choke down. This is something you learn by practice, but for any chip shot you should be choking down to some extent. As a result of this, you will be crouched more than for a full shot.

Your stance should be narrow. Now pull your left foot three or four inches from the flight line and at the same time *turn both feet some 30 to 45 degrees toward the target*. I want to stress angling the right foot as well as the left, something many players don't do. By pulling back your left foot and turning both feet, you free your legs to move smoothly and easily on the forward swing. Try squaring your stance and placing both feet perpendicular to your line of flight and notice how much more restricted your leg motion is.

Set about 70 percent of your weight on your left foot. Position the ball opposite your right toe. Actually, because your feet are turned, the ball will not be as far back in your stance as you think, but it will be back far enough to insure that your hands are set ahead of the ball. You want the feeling that the ball is back or to your right so that you are pulling the clubhead through the ball. Your blade should be square, aimed directly down your line of play, at address.

Your eyes should be approximately over the ball. You should feel that your body is slightly bowed toward the target. Don't exaggerate this, but feel that your knees and left hip are thrust toward the target and your left arm, shoulder and side are slightly extended. Your body would be in this bowed position at impact on a full shot. Place it in a similar position at address for the chip.

While your feet and hips are open to your intended line of play, *your shoulders should be square to that line*. This lets you swing your arms straight back and through and get the ball to the target.

The backswing is nothing more than a swinging back of the arms, with the left hand and arm in control and the hands and wrist remaining firm. I didn't say stiff or rigid. They should be relaxed but firm, with very little independent hand action and absolutely no flippiness. Just swing your arms back as far as you need to strike the ball the distance you want. There really is no movement at all in the legs.

When you have reached the end of your backswing and are ready

Use legs in chipping

Leg action is an overlooked but vital factor in the chipping stroke. With a minimum of wrist action and a firm left hand-arm position at impact, a soft, cushiony flow of the knees toward the target (pictures 4 through 7) gives you the feeling of pulling the club through the ball, just as on a full shot. Note that the feel for the shot, the "hit," is with the right hand, but with a set wrist so the right does not overpower the left and ruin the shot.

Swing straight back and through

The chip shot as seen from this angle is simply a movement of the arms and club straight back and straight through the ball, down the target line. Depending on the length of the stroke, the arms and clubhead may swing a little inside the target line on the backswing, but this is a natural result of the turning of the upper body and is not something you need worry about.

to start forward, there should be a slight movement forward with the legs. A flowing, cushiony movement with the knees will give you the feeling you are pulling the club through the ball just as you do on a full shot. Your hands are ahead of the clubhead and your weight is already on your left side. This lets you swing forward on the correct descending angle and strike the ball before you strike the turf. Now all you have to do is swing your arms forward through the ball, extending beyond it with hardly any hand action.

I can't overemphasize the importance of the correct leg action. It's what keeps your hands out of the shot and gives you the necessary feel. Remember, use no leg action as you swing your arms back. Then make a soft, flowing movement of the legs forward to start your arms swinging through the ball in firm-wristed fashion. Practice the motion—in your back yard, in your living room, everywhere—until the feeling of it is ingrained.

A message here about the right hand in the chipping stroke—use it. Heretical as that sounds from one so firmly committed to controlling the swing with the left side, I mean it and there's a reason for it. *You have a much better feel for distance with the right hand.* So control the swing with your left hand and arm, and feel you are striking the ball with your right. *But do that with a set wrist.* Don't flip the right hand at the ball. Swing it through without any hinging or unhinging of the wrist.

The chip shot takes sensitivity. What keeps most players from executing it well is tension. Professionals make it look simple because they stay relaxed. Our legs are relaxed. Our grip pressure is light. Our arms are relaxed and hanging down, not reaching. Our posture is good. All that lets us make the fluid, relaxed movement that the chip requires. If you have tension in your body, it interferes with natural swinging motion and ruins your tempo. The arms speed up, the legs lock and the hands take over, usually botching the shot.

So relax and trust your fundamentals to make the swing happen correctly.

Having come this far, you may now be wondering how to judge how hard to hit the chip shots of various lengths. The answer is proper practice.

When you practice chipping, do so with two things in mind. The first is to work on the basic stroke so you can make it with confidence in any situation. This will also help you develop a feel for your full-swing fundamentals. The second is to develop a feel for controlling the distance factor. Start your practice session by hitting a couple of dozen balls from one spot to one target, just working on your stroke. Then begin moving around. Shoot to different targets on the practice green. Move farther back from the edge of the green so you have carries of different lengths. Hit two balls to a target 15 feet away, then two to a target 60 feet

The longer the shot, the more lofted the club

Because Geiberger believes in using the chipping stroke from as far away as possible, landing the ball on the green as quickly as possible and letting it run to the hole, club selection becomes important. As shown here, the farther you are from the edge of the green and the hole, the more lofted your club must be (left) to provide a higher shot that lands more softly and will run a relatively shorter distance. From close in (right), you may use a less-lofted club that will get the ball down quickly and let it run to the hole.

away, then two more to a target 35 or 40 feet distant. Keep changing the distances in a random pattern. And never hit more than two balls in a row at one target, because after you have hit the first shot you know how hard to hit the next one. On the course, every chip you face will be of a different length. By changing your distances in practice, you make yourself figure out how hard to hit each particular shot. Soon you will know almost instinctively how big a swing to make for any given distance. *And remember that when you want to hit the ball farther, you simply make a longer swing, not necessarily a harder or faster one.*

Club selection is important in chipping. I'm not a believer in using just one club for all chip shots. In fact, with my system, you can't. I believe in using a basic chipping stroke whenever I'm as far away as 20 yards from the green. I prefer to roll the ball and not pitch it, if at all possible, because the percentages are better doing that than pitching it up in the air and having it bite one time and not the next.

The more like a putt you can make your shots around the green, the more consistently you can get them close to the hole. That's why I will chip the ball until I get so far away I simply have to get it up in the air with some spin to stop it in time. Until that point, I control distance and trajectory with club selection. I use the same swing and let the club do the work.

Your rule of thumb should be to take the club that will allow you to carry the ball *safely* on the green and let it run the rest of the way to the hole. Don't try to drop the ball just a foot past the apron. If you misjudge a little, it will land in the longer grass and wind up short every time. Allow yourself five or 10 feet of clearance, depending on your distance to the hole. Then if you misjudge your swing, you have a margin for error and a much better chance to get the ball close.

The variables you must consider in selecting a club are the distance needed to carry the ball to the putting surface and the amount of green available from the edge to the hole. Slope and speed of surface also must be factored in.

For example, if I'm just off the edge of the green on the short fringe, I might putt the ball, which is the safest shot of all. Whenever I'm in a close-in chipping situation, which means the intervening ground is too rough or the grass too long to putt over, and I have plenty of green to work with, I'll chip with a 6-iron. But from the same spot with the pin cut just 12 or 15 feet from the edge, I might use an 8-iron or even a pitching wedge, depending on whether I'm going uphill or downhill. I'm still playing a running-type shot with my chipping swing, but if I need more height to carry the ball farther or make the roll shorter, I just take a club with more loft. I don't try to manufacture height with a change in my swing. Making the same motion every time greatly enhances tempo and consistency.

RECAP—CHIPPING

SETUP

  Assume impact position at address.

● Flex knees.

● Bend from hips.

  Choke down on club.

  Open stance by pulling left foot back.

● Turn both feet 30–45 degrees toward target.

  Keep shoulders square to line of play.

● Set 70 percent of weight on left foot.

● Position ball off right foot, which puts hands ahead of clubhead.

  Align blade squarely at address.

  Set eyes over ball.

  Feel body is slightly bowed toward target.

  Relax!

SWING

  Swing left arm back, with no leg action, keeping wrist relaxed but firm.

  Initiate forward swing with an easy, flowing movement of the legs toward the target.

  Swing left arm forward, striking ball then turf and extending beyond. The hit and feel is with the right hand, but with a set wrist.

CLUB SELECTION

● Choose the least-lofted club that will land the ball safely on the green and let it run to the hole.

● Use your chipping stroke from as far away as possible. If you need more height on the shot, select a more-lofted club.

PRACTICE

● Work on the fundamentals of your basic stroke.

● Vary your distance, for both carry and roll, to teach your mind to relate how long your swing must be for shots of different lengths.

Pitch swing straight back and up, too

As with the full shot and the chip shot, you should feel on the pitch shot that you are swinging your arms straight back and up, then straight down and through on the forward swing.

Pitching

The pitch shot is just a bigger version of the chip shot. It is a high-flying shot that is used whenever you can't stop the ball near the hole with the chipping stroke. Normally it is played with a pitching wedge or sand wedge. Your pitching range is usually from 15 to 20 yards away—or closer when you don't have enough green to work with—on out to the point at which you must make a full swing.

The fundamentals of the pitching swing are virtually the same as those we discussed for the chipping stroke. Because it is a bigger swing, however, you need to take a slightly wider stance to keep your balance. And you should allow for a little more hand action, although not much, as I'll explain in a moment.

As with the chip shot, leg action on the forward swing is vital to the success of the pitch shot. Again I advocate that you angle both feet toward the target at address. This helps restrict your leg action on the backswing and encourages that easy, flowing movement that you want on the forward swing. As your swing gets longer, angle your feet less and square up your stance a little more. But keep the feet turned at least a little and your stance open a bit until you reach full-swing distance.

Because you want to hit this shot high most of the time, don't play the ball quite so far back in your stance. Position it about in the middle. This will keep your hands ahead of the ball, although not quite so much as on the chip shot.

The only other alteration that might be made for the pitch shot is in the position of your blade at address. While it is square or perpendicular to the line of play for a chip shot, you may want to open it—so that it is facing to the right of target—for pitching. It depends on how much height you need on the shot. The more you open the clubface, the more effective loft you add to it and the higher you will hit the pitch.

Those variations aside, you want to duplicate your chip-shot setup—knees flexed, upper body bent from the hips, arms hanging naturally, weight slightly toward the left side, stance and hips open, shoulders square, eyes over the ball and your body slightly bowed toward the target, set in a simulation of the impact position.

The swinging motion is the same but longer. Swing the club straight back and up, just as on the full shot. Because the swing is longer, there will be more turning of the shoulders. There will even be some lower body movement on the longer pitches as the arms pull the legs around. The longer swing also will cause the hands to cock more fully than on the chip. This means they will come into play more on the forward swing, more closely approximating a full swing. But this should not be a conscious effort on your part. The forward swing is still initiated with that movement of the legs, which lets you pull the club through with your left arm and side in control. That forward movement of the legs and the swinging of the arms, not anything you do with your hands, is what gets the ball in the air.

The pitch is just a bigger chip shot

The pitch shot swing is simply a bigger version of that used for the chip. The arms swing back farther and there is more cocking of the hands (4), but there is the same soft, flowing movement of the legs through the forward swing (pictures 5 through 8) and the same firm left hand and arm position at impact (7).

Just as with the chip shot, when your legs fail to work correctly on the forward swing, your hands take over, ruining your tempo and your shot. So develop the feeling of letting the legs start the forward swing, then swinging the arms down and through the ball along the line of play. On the follow-through, you should feel that your arms are swinging more upward than with the chipping swing.

Perhaps even more than the chip, the pitch is a shot that requires feel. That's why it's so important that you are relaxed at address and stay relaxed and unhurried throughout the swing. Any tension or untimely quickness will cause you to come to grief.

That's also why success at pitching depends so much on practice. It is totally unlike the full swing, whether it be with the 9-iron or the 2-iron. You make the same basic swing, and the club determines how far the ball goes. With the pitch shot, the problem is distance—judging and acquiring a feel for it, then relating the length of your swing to how far the ball must go. This feel is more important than on the chip shot because the distance variation is much greater. You might have a 50-yard pitch one time, a 20-yard pitch the next, a 32-yard pitch the next; and you must acquire the touch that lets you get the ball near the hole from all those distances.

The first thing that happens to me when I take a vacation from golf is that I lose my feel for pitching. The full swing stays with me because I've done it for so long and so often, but that pitching touch goes in a hurry. That's why you and I and anyone else who wants to develop and maintain any skill with the pitch shot must practice it constantly, probably more than any other stroke.

Your practice routine should be similar to that for the chip shot, except that you should spend relatively more time on distance judgment than the fundamental swing. If you have the facility, pitch to a practice green from different distances, trying to land the ball on a certain spot, judging how it checks up or bounces and rolls. If you don't have a practice green to which you can pitch, pick out different spots on the practice range, or knock balls out different distances and pitch to them.

Again, don't hit more than two balls in a row to a given target because you are trying to teach your mind to instinctively recognize the distance for any given shot. That's what you will be facing on the course, so you want to simulate that on the practice range.

RECAP—PITCHING

Fundamentals of the pitching swing are the same as for the chipping swing, except:

- Stance widens as the swing gets longer.

- Stance gets squarer with feet less angled as swing gets longer.

- Ball positioned in middle of stance.

- Open your clubface, depending on how high you want to hit the shot.

- Hands cock more on backswing and come into play more on forward swing, but only because swing is longer; there should be no conscious effort to use hands.

- Arms swing back and up, left arm and hand in control, on backswing; leg motion initiates forward swing, letting arms swing down and through ball and *up* to the finish.

- Relax!

- Practice, mainly from different distances.

Swing from outside to in when in sand

From the sand, swing somewhat along the line on which your body is set, which is open or to the left of your target. This outside-in path lets the rounded flange or "bounce" of the sand wedge work correctly. By opening the clubface and keeping it open through the swing, the ball will tend to come out to the right of your swing line and bounce toward the target.

Sand Play

There may be no place where good tempo is more important than in a greenside sand trap. Yet there may be no place where anxiety and tension interfere more with good tempo than in that same bunker. Most amateurs are deathly afraid of a shot from the sand, and that fear translates into tension.

The truth of the matter is, there is more margin for error in the sand than if you are hitting a pitch or chip shot from grass. In those situations you have to strike the ball precisely. In the sand, because you are not trying to strike the ball itself but the sand behind and underneath the ball, you can miss your shot with the clubhead by an inch or more and still get a satisfactory result.

Remember that. More than anything else, realizing that you have so much margin for error should relieve your anxiety, bolster your confidence and improve your tempo immeasurably.

As with every other shot in golf, especially the short strokes, the successful bunker shot depends on feel. That means you need the same good fundamentals, which lead to the same good tempo, that you use in the other swings. You also have to practice as much in the sand to develop the feel for distance and the different types of shots.

The single most valuable thought you can carry with you into a sand trap is to *finish the swing*. In the outings that I conduct and the pro-ams in which I play, I see too many players leave the club stuck in the sand. One reason is that they are afraid to swing through to the finish because they think they will knock the ball over the green. But I think the main reason is that these golfers have neglected the fundamentals, mainly good posture and good use of the legs, that have so much bearing on success in sand. With that in mind, let's look at those fundamentals one more time with an eye toward the changes you need to make in the sand.

I'll start by saying that *you don't need to make a fancy swing in a sand trap. Except for some important modifications in your setup, use the same swing you make in chipping and pitching.*

Your posture should be basically the same for the sand shot as it is for the other short shots—knees flexed, bent from the hips so arms are hanging, weight evenly distributed or slightly to your left, legs thrust slightly to the target. Work your feet into the sand to a depth of a couple of inches or so to get a firm base. This means you must also choke down on the club a couple of inches to maintain the same ball-club-feet relationship.

Because you will be striking the sand two inches or so behind the

Swing to a high finish on the sand shot

The setup and swing for the sand shot is basically the same as that for the pitch shot, except that you want to strike the sand two or three inches behind the ball.

Keeping the left hand and arm going firmly through impact and making a flowing movement of the legs is vital. Perhaps the most important thought is to finish the swing, making your hands go high on the follow-through. This promotes left-side firmness and acceleration through the shot.

3

4

7

8

ball, play the ball more forward in your stance than for a normal pitch shot—just off the inside of your left heel is a good guideline, but you should experiment to find the right position for you.

The other basic difference in address for sand play is that your feet *and* shoulders should be set in an open position. Pull the left foot six or seven inches back from the square position. For the chip shot, you'll remember, your shoulders were set parallel to your line of play. For the sand shot, they should be parallel with your stance line. Your clubface should be *open*, aimed at the flag or slightly to the right of the flag. From this set-up, your swing path will naturally follow the line of your shoulders, which will be to the left of the target. This path, combined with the slightly open clubface, lets the "bounce" of the club—the wide, rounded sole or bottom—work most effectively, riding through the sand on a shallow cut and helping lift the ball out on a cushion of sand.

As I said, there is no fancy work required when you swing. Aim at that spot a couple of inches or so behind the ball. In a relaxed manner, swing the left arm back and up, with little leg motion going back. Coming through, use your legs as I have described earlier. Without good leg action, your hands will take over, quickening your tempo and causing you to flip at the ball. When this happens, the club loses acceleration, the sand grabs the club and, if it doesn't stop it, slows it down to the point where you lose all power and leave the ball in the bunker.

When you practice sand shots, begin by taking full swings. Get the feeling of the ball coming out of the trap. Feel the clubhead slicing through the sand under the ball, and swing through to the finish. Don't worry about how far the ball goes for a while. Just feel the clubhead accelerating through the sand with a full swing.

Then begin to notice how far the ball is traveling as the result of a full swing. After you have determined the distance you're getting, start taking shorter swings for shorter shots until you get down to the little-bitty trap shot that you need to just lift the ball over the lip. Don't make your backswing so short that you feel forced to use your hands instead of your legs and arms to get clubhead speed. But a short backswing is better than one that is too long. When you swing back too far, your club is more likely to decelerate coming into the ball. Also, always make your follow-through at least as long as your backswing, and longer if you can. This is a good way to make sure your club is accelerating as you swing through the impact area.

We professionals get a small chuckle out of the amazed reactions we get on tour from galleries when we successfully play a bunker shot from a buried lie, a ball sunk at least partially below the surface of the sand. Actually, this is a fairly simple shot and can be played consistently and accurately to the hole if you have enough green to work with. Simply square up your stance a little, set your weight more to the left, square your blade and strike down into the sand a couple of inches behind the

NO   **YES**

ball, or at the edge of the crater it made when it buried.

As long as you accelerate aggressively through the sand—in some cases, if the ball is deep, you must feel as if you are burying the clubhead in the sand hard—the ball will come out. It won't have much spin on it and will run quite a way, but you can learn to judge that.

RECAP—SAND PLAY

Remember that there is more margin for error in the sand than on a chip or pitch shot.

The successful bunker shot depends on feel.

Your most important thought is to finish the swing.

Make the same basic swing that you make for a chip or pitch.

Fundamentals are the same as for a pitch, except stance is more open, shoulders are open and ball is played more forward.

With an open clubface, strike two inches or so behind the ball.

Swing the left arm going back and use good leg action coming forward.

Acceleration is the key: make your follow-through at least as long as your backswing.

For a buried lie, square your stance and blade and strike down at edge of crater in sand.

Don't let right overpower left in sand

If the right hand becomes too active on the sand shot, overpowering and breaking down the left hand (left), you are likely to bury the clubhead in the sand and probably leave the ball in the bunker. Instead, keep the left hand and arm moving solidly through the shot so the "bounce" of the club can work properly, sliding through the sand and lifting the ball out.

TEMPO ON THE GREEN

There are smarter people than I who will tell you that putting is the most important thing in the game, and I guess I wouldn't argue with that. If you are putting well, it fires you up mentally. If you miss a few shots, you don't panic. You usually get it up and down and think, "I'm hitting the ball well." Because you have holed some putts, you forget about those missed shots. But if you are putting poorly and you miss a couple of shots, those misses can ruin your round.

My concept of putting starts with getting comfortable. The setup—your grip, posture and alignment—is the key. If you are not in a good position, you can't be very natural . . . or consistent. In putting, as in every other shot, the better your fundamentals are, the more consistent you will be, the more confident you will be and the better your tempo will be. Poor fundamentals create anxiety and thus poor tempo. In putting, we call that the *yips*. But what you think are poor nerves and a natural lack of confidence is really just a result of improper fundamentals. It's a chain reaction that leads to disaster.

So let's take a close look at the fundamentals as they apply to putting.

Grip

The putting grip differs from the grip for other shots in that the hands are a little more "opposed"—the left hand is turned more to the left, the right hand more to the right. The handle of the putter is placed more against the heel pad of the left hand rather than under it. Ideally, it lies in the crevice between the two pads.

The last three fingers of the left hand close around the handle. The right hand is then placed on the club in an "opposed" position—turned as much to the right as the left hand is turned to the left. The V's formed by thumbs and forefingers should balance—a good guide is that each points to its respective shoulder, but that can vary to fit your individual characteristics. The forefinger of the left hand now fits over the fingers of

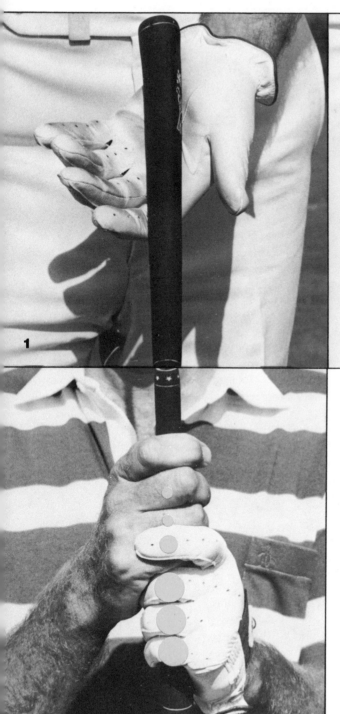

How to assume your putting grip

For the putting grip, the left hand is turned more to the left. The club lies from the base of the left forefingers up the palm and along the crevice between the heel and thumb pads (1). The last three fingers of the left hand are closed around the club (2) and the right hand is applied in an "opposed" position—turned as much to the right as the left hand is to the left (3 and 4). The left forefinger overlaps the fingers of the right hand. The pressure, as with the regular grip, is in the last three fingers of the left hand, with a little less pressure applied by the overlapped forefinger. There is just slight pressure in the two middle fingers of the right hand.

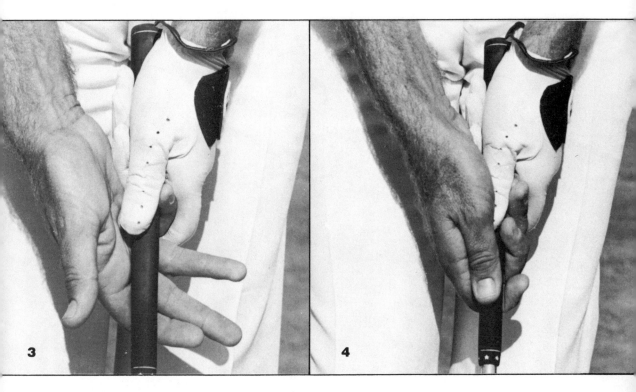

the right in what is known as the reverse overlap grip.

Grip pressure should be firm *without tension*, concentrated in the last three fingers of your left hand and the middle two fingers of your right. Relaxation is especially important in putting, and tension usually starts in the grip.

I put all four fingers and the thumb of my right hand on the club, but some players on tour use what is called the double overlap grip, overlapping the little finger of the right hand over the middle finger of the left while still reverse overlapping with the left forefinger. This serves to get the right hand higher on the club, and the higher you can get it, the better it will work in tandem with the left. Also, the higher the right hand, the less pressure it exerts on the clubhead, letting you more easily keep the face square during the stroke.

Experiment and see which grip works best for you.

Setup

Set your weight a little more on the left side because that creates the feeling that you are stroking slightly downward on the putt. It helps avoid the tendency to raise up with the stroke and fail to strike the ball solidly.

Position the ball anywhere from just inside your left heel to just

1   YES   2   NO

ahead of the center of your stance. Any farther back than that will promote a tendency to *pinch* the ball against the turf too much. Spotting the ball farther forward than the left heel makes it harder to keep your hands ahead of the putterhead where they belong.

I set my feet square to the line, although this is not as important in putting as in the other shots. Flex your knees a little and bend from the hips just enough to let your arms hang naturally. Try to stay as erect or "high" as possible; this lets your arms hang better and gives you a better swinging motion. If you reach for the ball, you will take the putter back too *flat* or around your body and won't be able to keep it on line as well. You will ruin the pendulum effect you want in your swing.

Because the ball is so much closer to you in putting—it should be on a line directly under your eyes—your arms will not hang straight. There is a relaxed inward bend to them, your elbows almost brushing against your sides. Then arch your wrists, which creates a zig-zag look

3   **NO**

Set eyes over line, let arms hang

Your putting posture should be such that your eyes are positioned over your target line and your arms are hanging comfortably (1). Arch your wrists for added firmness. If your eyes are set outside the target line (2) or inside it (3), your aim will be distorted and the pendulum effect in your swing will be hampered.

to arms and hands from the side and creates the firmness needed.

  The amount of arm bend and knee flex depends to a great extent on your height. A shorter player like Ben Crenshaw, who may be one of the best putters ever, can stand relatively straight-legged and let his left arm hang straight down in a relaxed manner. A tall player like George Archer, who is 6–6 and a very, very good putter, must crouch more, bending at the hips, knees and elbows to make everything work. It's almost as if the zig-zag in the arms balances out with the zig-zag in the hips and knees.

  The determining factor for you is to grip the putter and get into a position in which your eyes are over the target line while your arms are hanging just free of your torso. Everything else will fall into place.

  Balance is important in your putting setup. If one elbow is close to your side, the other should be. If the right elbow is akimbo, the left should be also. That's why you want the hands opposed—either in the neutral

position or set with the V's pointing the same degree in opposite directions. The body plays no part in putting, so you want to make your stroke as much like a pendulum as possible. To do this, all elements must be in balance.

Even more than in the full swing, your eye alignment is crucial in putting. You'll recall my Bud Palmer story in which I noted that his clubface lined up with the tilt of his face. The same thing holds true in putting, and because it is a shorter, more critical shot, the results can be even more disastrous.

If your eyes are cocked to the right, which is the common problem, you invariably will aim the blade to the right and pull it back inside your correct target line. Then you must do something to get it back on line to the hole. Either you push the putt to the right or you bring the right hand too much into play and pull it to the left.

So make sure your eyeline is set straight with the target line. Then

Keep eye-line square

For best aiming and stroking, your eyes should be set square to or parallel with your target line (1). A common fault is to tilt or cock them to the right, which will tend to alter your blade alignment (2). When you look at your line and the target, keep your eye-line square by rotating your head and eyes back and forth (3) instead of lifting your head.

rotate your head and eyes back and forth while viewing the line and the cup. Don't lift your head and get your eyeline askew. And after you strike the putt, rotate your head and eyes, keeping them square with the line as you follow the ball to the hole. This teaches you proper visual perspective and will help you in lining up future putts.

The Stroke

I had a bad putting streak several years ago, putting poorly for two or three years. Finally, I began going to the putting green and watching all the good putters—Jack Nicklaus, Ben Crenshaw, Dave Stockton and others. I told myself that there had to be some common denominators among them. I checked their postures, their stances, their grips, everything, and I finally discovered the one thing they all had in common—the left wrist. They all moved it a little differently. Some set up with it in a

"Eliminate" the left wrist

Ideally, the putting stroke should be made in a firm-wristed fashion, allowing no breakdown of the left hand. The stroke is made with the arms, similar to the action of a pendulum, making no special manipulations to keep the putterhead low. With your hands set slightly ahead of the ball, take the putter back with your left hand in control. The right hand comes into play on the forward stroke, providing the feel for distance, but the left wrist remains firm throughout the stroke.

different position. Some hinged it a little going back. But as they were coming through, *each looked as if he didn't have a left wrist.*

Since then I've come to the conclusion that we all would be better putters if we didn't have a left wrist. Since that's not the case—and it might wreak havoc with the rest of your game, anyway—we have to concentrate on a technique that will keep that left wrist as straight and firm as possible through the forward stroke. This insures little or no variance in the left hand, and since anything that the left hand does is reflected by a movement of the putterface, you want to keep it as solid as possible. This is why some players who are having trouble go to a cross-handed style—that grip automatically arches and firms the left wrist.

Again, I'd suggest you experiment to find the best way for you to do this. There certainly are a variety of techniques on the tour. Nicklaus lets his left arm hang almost straight down with a very high left shoulder, setting his upper body behind the ball in a noticeable crouch. His left arm and putter are almost one, a straight line. Then he uses his right hand and arm in a piston-like fashion.

Dave Stockton, long one of the best putters on tour, breaks or hinges his left wrist a little going back, then keeps it solid as he pulls through on the forward stroke. His theory is that he just keeps his left hand going to the hole, and this sets up everything else in the stroke.

Lou Graham, also a good putter, does it a little differently. He sets his left elbow akimbo towards the hole, which breaks his left wrist right at the start. Then he just pushes his right hand against his left coming through, and because the left wrist is already hinged, it can't break down anymore. So Lou is achieving the same effect.

There have been great putters whose left wrists did hinge during the stroke. Billy Casper is a prime example. He has been strictly a hands putter all his life, and he's been a great one. But he hinges his hands straight back and straight through, and like Lou Graham he really doesn't break down his left wrist as much as it appears. It already is broken at address and he just hits against it. He doesn't really move the left forearm and wrist very much during a stroke.

Arnold Palmer, certainly one of the great pressure putters in his prime, always used a combination arm-and-hand stroke. But there are a lot of variables in that kind of action, and it may have caught up with Arnold. Later in his career, poor putting became his big problem.

Frank Beard is a similar example. A million-dollar winner and once one of the great putters on tour, he always had a wristy right-handed stroke, taking the blade back inside the line and closing it as he came through, all the time working with a bad eye alignment. That worked fine while he had his confidence, but once some things started to go wrong and he began to doubt himself, all those variables came into play, and he has had trouble getting back on the track.

What I am proposing is that you eliminate the variables. The more of them you get rid of in your stroke, the better putter you will be. When you are choking under pressure, and maybe your tempo is getting a little quick, you want to be able to move the putterhead to the hole with as simple an action as possible. Bobby Nichols, for example, can mis-hit more putts and still make them more often than anybody I've ever seen. He controls the putter with his arms, not his hands, and while he has a tendency to come up on putts and mis-hit them, he mis-hits them straight. You can see by his reaction when he thinks he has left a crucial

Stroke straight back and through

On shorter putts, the stroke is essentially straight back and straight through to the target. For long putts, the clubhead will begin to swing inside the target line going back and the face will appear to fan open. This is natural because of the turning of the shoulders—your sensation still should be that of swinging straight back and through.

putt short, but it will keep going into the hole. If your hands get too active, though, you have very little chance to keep the face square and the putt on line under pressure.

The guidelines I've mentioned are fairly basic, but experiment within the context of your own capabilities and experiences to find the style of putting that is right for you—as long as that left wrist remains firm.

To achieve firmness in the left hand and wrist, make sure your hands are set slightly ahead of the ball and that there is an arch in your wrists, mentioned earlier. This will give you firmness without tension, without having to squeeze the club.

In the spring of 1979 I had not been playing well, and most of it was because of poor putting. At the Byron Nelson Classic, the day before I missed the cut, I was working on the putting green and a friend of mine pointed out that my hands were set behind the ball at address. They had crept back there without my being aware of it. As a result, I was not able to keep the left wrist firm coming through the stroke and the right hand was taking over.

Later, I discovered that I was not arching my wrists the way I had in the past. This was another factor in creating a sloppy stroke. So I made sure to keep my wrists arched and keep my hands set slightly ahead of the putterhead—thumbs over the ball is a good guideline—and the results were a little more spectacular than I could have imagined. I won the Colonial National Invitation the next week with some of the best putting I'd had in a long time.

You may not achieve results like that so quickly, but in the long run your putting will improve. With the arms hanging down in relaxed fashion and the arching of your wrists giving you firmness without tension, you achieve the best possible position from which to make the stroke.

The actions of the left and right hands are the same in putting as they are in chipping. The left hand and arm control the swing, remaining firm throughout. But it is not totally a left-side stroke. The right hand plays a big part in putting. As in chipping, it is the instrument you use to determine how hard you are going to hit the putt. It is the hand that gives you the feel for the correct distance. But as in chipping, once the right hand is set in position at address, it should remain in that position throughout. There should be no flippiness, no change in position of the right hand or arm, coming through the stroke. Your right hand hits against the firm left hand and arm and lets you roll the ball the correct distance to the hole. I am a stroke rather than a jab putter. I feel my putter continues on down the line after I strike the ball rather than coming to an abrupt stop or jabbing into the turf. I like to make my follow-through at least as long as my backswing. When I putt badly, it usually is because my putterhead stops just past the ball.

The stroke is initiated with the left hand and arm swinging back in unison. That causes a rocking of the shoulders, which is all the body movement you want. If your body moves, it not only causes the club-head to wobble off-line but also encourages deceleration. It is the same as on a full shot—once the upper body moves, you lose some of the centrifugal force that is building up in your swing. Some players and teachers advocate thinking of putting with the shoulders, but I find this induces too much body movement. Putting with the arms accomplishes the same thing, because the arms swinging will cause the shoulders to move correctly.

Here's a tip. Start your stroke with the putterhead a fraction off the ground. That makes it easier to start the backswing because you don't meet any resistance from the grass, and that in turn smooths out your tempo. I happen to put the putterhead on the ground while I'm lining up the putt, then pick it up slightly just before I start the stroke. Jack Nicklaus, among others, never grounds the putterhead.

The putterhead should be kept reasonably low to the ground during the stroke, but not artificially so. Remember, it's a pendulum action, a miniature swing, so you should make no unnatural movement to keep the head low too far into the backswing or the follow-through. It will naturally rise somewhat at both ends of the stroke. Just swing your arms while keeping your hands and wrists firm and you will achieve the correct arc.

The same rule applies to the path of your club. You want to try to swing the club straight back and through with your arms, but on the longer strokes it will naturally come a bit inside the target line on your backswing. Then it will move back onto and down the line and inside again on the forward stroke. That's because your arms are swinging a little bit around your body on the longer strokes.

By the same token, the clubface will appear to open just a little on the backswing and close again coming through. That's because your hands and forearms are rotating slightly as they swing back and through.

None of this should concern you. Don't try to make any compensations to keep the putterhead on line or the face square to the line. Just think of swinging the arms back and through and let everything else happen naturally. When I shot the 59, I felt I was taking the putter back on a straight line and through on a straight line. It began to feel better and better, my confidence began to rise, my tempo got better and my stroke got smoother. It's something that just builds when you establish a technique based on correct fundamentals.

Acceleration in the putting stroke is as important as it is in any other shot. The ruination of acceleration is taking the putter back too far, because you instinctively know that if you accelerate from that position you would hit the ball too far. So you decelerate coming through, usually failing to strike the ball solidly or on line.

You may find that your right hand is causing you to take the putter back too far. This means you have allowed it to take over from the left. Put the stroke back in control of the left hand and arm. Your stroke will automatically get shorter, your tempo will improve and you will start making more putts.

Take the putter back a distance that relates to the length of the putt. That will maintain the proper pace or tempo of your putting stroke. I can't tell you how far that would be for you. As with any other phase of the short game, it is something you must learn from practice, by practicing putts of all distances on the putting green until you can instinctively match the feel and length of your stroke to the length of your putt.

When I get excited, I have a tendency to take the putter back too fast, and I'm sure it is no different for most players, professional or amateur. Then it is hard to maintain any consistent tempo. Your stroke gets loose and wristy and you more than likely will instinctively decelerate coming forward. You lose the acceleration that keeps your clubhead moving down the line.

The answer, I find, is that when I'm under pressure I try to swing the club back as slowly as possible. Not artificially so, however. Johnny Miller used to take it back almost in a two-piece movement. He would almost stop, then start again. He won the U. S. Open doing that, but I don't recommend it for those of us who are less talented, because you lose the rhythmic feel you need for good putting. Swing it back with good tempo so you can anticipate the buildup of acceleration on the forward swing.

RECAP—PUTTING

Grip with the hands opposed.

Set weight slightly left.

Bend from hips so arms hang freely but close to body.

Ball is played on a line directly under your eyes.

Arms are slightly bent.

Wrists arched and hands ahead of ball for firmness.

Eyes aligned squarely with target line.

Stay relaxed at address and throughout the stroke.

Putt as if you have no left wrist.

Control stroke with left hand and arm, but hit with right hand for distance feel.

Swing with arms, not hands or shoulders.

Swing arms straight back and through, allowing putterhead to travel on its natural arc and path.

Maintain acceleration by not taking putter back too far.

Practice different length putts to develop distance judgment.

Swing the putter back slowly, with good tempo.

FINESSE SHOTS AND TROUBLE SHOTS

Now that you are familiar with my fundamentals of the golf swing—and hopefully will practice them enough to develop some proficiency—you must learn to put them to work in playing situations. This means not only applying the fundamentals to hit normal shots but also to finesse the ball, to hit shots of different shapes, distances and trajectories, from slopes and from various lies.

Good tempo is particularly important in hitting finesse shots, because you are doing something out of the ordinary—changing your setup and maybe making a slight change in your swing. But the important thing to remember is that your fundamentals don't change. If you trust your fundamentals, you will have the confidence to maintain a smooth tempo no matter what kind of shot you are making.

Learning to hit these special shots accomplishes a couple of things. Most important, it lets you play better. Not only can these shots save you strokes, they also help you develop a feel for the game. Golf is a game of changing situations, and you probably need to hit more "special" shots than normal ones on the course. Every shot has a different feel, whether it is because of your lie, the wind, the atmosphere, a tree blocking your path or simply the way you yourself feel. By learning to hit different shots, you can better adjust to these different feels and cope with them successfully.

Learning the finesse shots also will tell you something about your swing. If you can successfully hit fades and draws and other cute shots, it means your swing is fundamentally correct. If you can't, you had better start reviewing those fundamentals to find out where you are going wrong.

The basic finesse shots are the fade, which moves from left to right; the draw, which moves from right to left; the high shot and the low shot; the shots from various slopes; and the shots from rough and fairway traps. The slice is a pronounced fade and the hook is a pronounced draw. There may be times when you want to deliberately hit those, and doing so is just a matter of accentuating what I am going to tell you.

Fade | **Straight**

1 | 2

My description of how to hit these shots is going to be brief, which might surprise you. It shouldn't, because the modifications required to hit these shots are really very simple. Just keep in mind that the fundamentals which apply to a normal shot apply as well to these shots.

Fade—Draw

To hit the *fade*—to move the ball from left to right—aim your clubface at the target, then open your stance and your hip and shoulder alignment—set your body a bit to the left. Now make your normal swing, the path of which will follow your body alignment. The only swing change you make is that you "hold on" a little more through the impact area— you keep the back of the left hand firmer and going more toward the target instead of releasing and rotating as it would in a normal shot. A full rotation and release would tend to close the clubface and make you pull

Draw

3

Alter setup for fade, draw

To curve the ball intentionally, simply keep the clubface aimed at your target and alter your address position. For a left-to-right fade (1), set your feet and body to the left of your target and swing along your stance line. "Hold on" a bit through impact, not allowing your hands to release or turn over as much as they normally would. For the right-to-left draw (3), set your feet and body to the right. Allow your hands to release fully and cross over as you swing through impact. For the straight shot (2), the feet and body are aligned parallel to your target line.

the ball left in the direction of your swing path.

If you want to *draw* the ball, your setup and swing action will be just the opposite. Close your stance and body alignment a bit, drawing your right foot a few inches back from the line and aligning your body accordingly. Keep your clubface aimed at the target. As you swing, be sure you stay behind the ball with your upper body so you will swing on the inside-to-out path your body alignment has dictated. This time you want to make a full release, an accentuated rotation of the hands and forearms as you swing through impact.

With either of these shots, the amount of curve that you obtain in the flight of the ball is something you must learn by practice. There is no formula that will tell you precisely what you must do to make the ball curve a precise distance. As with any other facet of the golf game, it is a learned process that comes through experimentation on both the practice tee and the course, a matter of feel that you must incorporate into

Low

High

Alter ball position for high, low shots

To set up for a low shot (left), play the ball well back in your stance and keep your hands ahead. For the high shot (right), play the ball farther forward than normal with your hands slightly behind the ball and your weight set more to the right.

your game.

There are some teachers and players who advocate changing the grip to effect a fade or draw—weakening it by turning both hands to the left for the fade, strengthening it by turning them to the right for a draw. That can work, and it may be something you would want to experiment with. My personal belief is that a grip adjustment is more awkward than changing your setup, and the sense of discomfort that results could interfere with your swing fundamentals. I like to keep it as simple as possible, so I leave the grip alone.

Low—High

To hit the *low* shot, keeping the ball down into the wind or under some tree branches, there is one important element that most players overlook—*it is usually not a full shot*. The shot should be struck with something less than a complete swing, because a full, hard blow will impart too much backspin, causing the ball to rise more than you want. The good wind players are those who are able to adapt their tempo and make 80 percent or 90 percent swings. They can hit the soft shot, which is what you need to do in the wind, even though your instincts tell you to hit the ball harder. The low shot should be more of a "bump" shot, for which you take more club than you would normally need and bump the ball to your target.

The technique is simple. Play the ball back in your stance so you will strike it with the clubface in a delofted or hooded position. How far back depends on how low you want to hit the shot. Choke down on the club a little and take a three-quarter swing. Make sure your hands stay ahead of the clubhead, and as you swing through, don't release. Don't allow your hands and arms to turn over. Simply think of having your hands ahead of the clubhead at address and keeping them there to the finish. This will give you the low, running trajectory you want. One warning—don't let your upper body creep ahead of the ball so your legs won't work and you raise up on the shot, maybe topping it.

For the *high* shot, when you need to clear a tree, move the ball forward in your stance a couple of inches. You must have a good lie, with a cushion of grass underneath your ball, or you are liable to skull the shot. Set your weight slightly more to the right. Now just make a good full swing, with good leg action and good arm swing through the ball. The shot will sail much higher than normal.

Maintaining good tempo is very important on this shot. It's easy to try to hit the high shot too hard because you want to send the ball higher than usual and still carry it to your target, and you instinctively feel you don't have enough club to do that. Here's a hint that may help. On many occasions I have found myself in a situation where, say, an 8-iron is the only club that will get my ball over a tree, but it's not enough club to get the ball to the green. So I take the 8-iron anyway, hit the shot, and much to my surprise I knock the ball on the green. The reason is that in trying to hit the shot high, my legs were working better. I made a much better release through the ball, so I hit it farther than normal. The same can work for you. Just make a full, smooth swing at a good pace and the ball will go higher and farther than you expect.

Both the high and low shots require practice and experimentation to learn just where you should play the ball and how hard or soft you should swing. You have to learn for yourself just what the ball will do from a particular position in your stance.

Uphill and Downhill Lies

Playing from sloping lies is basically a matter of adjusting your ball

Uphill

Downhill

Change ball position for uphill, downhill lies

On an uphill lie, position the ball more forward in your stance and remember that the shot will tend to fly shorter and to the left. From a downhill lie, put the ball back in your stance and allow for the shot to travel, lower, farther and to the right.

position and weight distribution. For uphill and downhill lies, especially, that adjustment becomes simpler if you think of the swing as a circle and relate that circle to the slope. On an uphill lie, your clubhead is going to make contact with the ground later in the circle, so you want to play the ball forward in your stance. On a downhill lie, the club is going to make contact earlier in the circle, so the ball should be moved back in your stance. How much forward or back depends on the severity of the slope. This you learn by experience.

Because of the slopes, your weight is going to tend to be more toward your right foot on an uphill lie and more toward your left foot on a downhill lie. Other than that, you don't make any significant changes in your setup or swing.

What you must take into account is the effect the slopes will have on your ball flight. An uphill lie has the effect of creating more loft in a club. A 7-iron becomes an 8-iron and the ball will fly higher and shorter. You also

Sidehill

will tend to pull the ball left from an uphill lie. A downhill lie delofts the clubface so your 8-iron becomes a 7-iron. The ball will travel lower, hotter and will go farther. It also may tend to tail off to the right. If you figure in these variables before you make the shot, you'll be able to handle these lies with little difficulty.

Sidehill Lies

For sidehill lies, use the same circle theory in a slightly different way. If the ball is above your feet, the circle of your swing will be more tilted, or flatter, in relation to the horizon. You'll want to choke down on the club a little to partially compensate for this, but your arc still will be flatter and coming more from the inside into the hill. For this reason, you will contact the ground earlier than usual, so play the ball back in your stance. Because of the arc and swing path, you will tend to hook the ball, or

Adjust aim from sidehill lies

When the ball is below your feet (left), position it normally or slightly forward in your stance and aim to the left to allow for a fade to the right. When the ball is above your feet (right), play it back in your stance and aim to the right to allow for a hook to the left.

Swing steeper from fairway trap

From a fairway sand trap, set up with a slightly open stance, swing back (1) and down (2) on a steeper-than-normal angle, taking the club back slightly outside your target line (3) and allowing for a left-to-right fade. Be sure you contact the ball first.

pull-hook it to the left, so compensate by aiming more to the right. If there are trees that prevent aiming to the right and you must hit the ball as straight as possible, open your clubface to compensate for the other factors.

If the ball is below your feet, your circle will be more upright or more vertical to the horizon. Play the ball where you normally would, or slightly forward, but aim your body and clubface to the left to allow for the left-to-right action you will get. Again, if you can't aim left, close your clubface to overcome the slicing tendency.

Whether the ball is above or below your feet, your posture still should be based on letting your arms hang naturally with the weight as much as possible toward the balls of your feet.

The Fairway Bunker Shot

Playing from fairway sand traps is not as difficult as many golfers make it. You want to contact the ball first, just as with a normal fairway shot, but you can't make quite a normal level swing for fear of hitting the sand first and killing the shot.

Simply make sure your feet are securely anchored in the sand, take a slightly open stance with the left foot pulled back, choke down on the club a little to counteract the fact that your feet are partially buried, and play the ball in its normal position or slightly forward of normal. Then swing the club up more sharply or steeply than you normally would, slightly to the outside of your target line. I feel almost like I'm fanning the club open a little as I swing it up. Then swing down through the ball on a steeper-than-normal angle, making certain you strike the ball first. I feel as if I'm hitting a "cut" shot or a deliberate fade. The steeper angle and a slightly open clubface will cause the ball to rise more quickly than usual. It also will cause the ball to fade from left to right, so you must allow for this when you aim.

You will lose from a half to one club's worth of distance with this type of shot, so take more club than the distance calls for. But there is one vital rule of club selection—always take a club with enough loft to get you over the lip of the bunker. If the 6-iron is the only club that will get the ball over the lip, don't take a 5. Take the 6 and leave yourself short of the green, if you have to. The worst thing you can do is leave the ball in the trap and have the shot to make all over again.

With practice, you'll soon be able to figure how much your shots are going to curve and how quickly you can get the ball in the air with various clubs, so your club selection and aim will become much easier.

The Shot From Rough

The full shot from rough is basically the same as that from the fairway

Swing steeper from rough

Just as when you are in a fairway bunker, you should steepen your swing arc when your ball lies in heavy grass. Line up in a slightly open stance (1), then pick the club up more sharply (2) and bring it down on a steeper angle (3) to avoid, as much as possible, getting your clubhead tangled in the grass.

bunker. Set up with your stance slightly open; take the club up more sharply and to the outside as you fan it open a bit; then drop the club down on the ball at a steeper angle. That keeps too much grass from catching the club as it comes into the ball and also pops the ball up more quickly, which means it has less chance of catching in the grass. This shot will not slice as much as the shot from the bunker because any grass that gets between the clubface and ball will reduce the spin.

Again, the shot from rough requires a lot of practice. You must learn to judge the thickness of the grass and the lowest-numbered club you can use to get the ball out. As with the fairway bunker shot, don't force a less-lofted club. If you judge that a 7-iron is needed to get out of the grass, don't use a 5- or 6-iron, because you risk leaving the ball in the rough. The first requirement is to get back on the fairway, even if you can't reach the green. Besides, you might be surprised at how much distance you can get with a more-lofted club. Because the grass will

reduce spin, the ball will roll farther than normal and you might get pretty close to the green.

One caution—seldom, if ever, should you use a long iron out of heavy grass. If that much distance is needed, you're much better off going with one of the more lofted fairway woods. The head shape of a wood allows it to slide through the grass better without getting tangled and you are more apt to get the ball out and in the vicinity of the green.

Finally, from lighter rough especially, it's good to be aware of a phenomenon we call the "flyer." This is a shot that usually travels farther than normal because some grass gets trapped between clubface and ball and reduces the spin. What occurs then is a knuckleball effect that causes the ball to carry and roll farther than you expect. Sometimes you play for a flyer and don't get it, coming up short. At other times it happens unexpectedly. About all you can do is learn from experience when the shot is likely to occur so you can be as ready as possible.

The Short Pitch From Rough

For the shot out of rough from 15 or 20 yards and in, the key is *acceleration*. Mechanically, the shot is a cross between the normal pitch shot and the greenside sand shot. Address it with an open stance, your weight toward the left side and the ball played a little farther back in your stance than you would for the sand shot. This gives you more of a descending blow, which you need.

I prefer to use a sand wedge for this shot because of its extra weight and broader flange or bottom, which helps it slide through the grass better. Keep the blade more square than you would for a normal pitch shot, unless you need to open it a little to pop up the ball more quickly. But be careful not to get it too open or you might cut right underneath the ball.

Because there probably is grass wrapped around the ball, try to strike a little behind the ball, although not as much as you would for a sand shot. Let the ball fly out on a cushion of grass. Playing this shot successfully is greatly dependent on experience and your ability to judge the consistency of the grass, so the more you practice it the better off you will be. It's also a good idea to take two or three practice swings before each shot to get a feel for the grass.

Again, you must accelerate through the shot, just as in the bunker shot. If you decelerate and quit going through, the grass wins and tangles your club. Even on a short shot from the edge of the green, you must have the club traveling with enough force to pop the ball out. As with the normal pitch or chip, good leg action combined with a good arm swing is essential to accomplish this acceleration.

Those are the basic finesse shots. Practice them on the range and work with them on the course. There also are many other shots that you can learn to hit—half shots, three-quarter shots, soft lobs, low runners. The best way to learn these is to go to the course in the evening and play with just three or four clubs. Make those clubs take the place of a full set by changing the way you use them. Make your 5-iron go 7-iron distance, that sort of thing. Not only will you have a lot of fun, you also can learn to play this game.

RECAP—FINESSE SHOTS

● Fade—aim clubface at target, set body to left and swing normally with less forearm rotation.

● Draw—aim clubface at target, set body to right and swing normally with full forearm rotation and release.

● Low shot—play ball back in stance and make three-quarter swing without releasing fully.

● High shot—play ball forward, set weight more to right and make a full swing.

● Uphill lie—play ball forward, take more club and allow for flight to left.

● Downhill lie—play ball back, take less club and allow for flight to right.

● Ball above feet—play ball back, allow for right-to-left ball flight.

● Ball below feet—play ball in normal position, or slightly forward, and allow for left-to-right flight.

● From fairway bunker—play ball slightly forward, open stance slightly, make a steeper, outside-in swing; take club with enough loft to clear lip; allow for fade.

● From fairway rough—open stance, make a steeper, outside-in swing; use enough loft to get out of grass.

● From greenside rough—play ball slightly back, use sand wedge with square blade, strike grass slightly behind ball and be sure to accelerate through shot.

TRAINING FOR BETTER TEMPO

Having emphasized throughout this book the value of practice, I think it's only fair to tell you how to practice and how to prepare for a round of golf.

I am often asked how many practice balls I hit a day —100? 500? 1,000? The stories are legion about tour players who beat hundreds of balls daily, practicing for hours until their hands are cracked and bleeding, and I guess people believe them. Actually, we do have some legendary practicers—guys like Tom Watson and Tom Kite and Lee Trevino have been known to practice for several hours at a time, especially if they are having some problems or are working on something in particular. And any professional worth his salt has to spend *some* time on the practice tee each day.

But have you every tried to hit 500 golf balls? I got to about 400 one day, including a lot of wedge shots, and almost collapsed.

Actually, I think a lot of practice at one time can be just as harmful as no practice at all, especially for a beginning player or the average amateur who doesn't have the strength and stamina that a tour professional does. Too much practice is particularly damaging to your tempo. I know that after I've been home for a while and am getting ready to go back out on tour, I help my tempo more just by hitting balls a short time each day instead of beating out a lot at a time. Once I get on that second bag of balls and start hitting my driver, my tempo gets faster and faster. I tell myself to slow down, but I can't.

So I think that once you get past your first bucket of balls, the first half hour or so, you not only are wasting your time but are in danger of undoing all the good you had done before. You will start to get tired, you will begin to swing harder, and your tempo goes out the window.

If you want to practice longer than that, take a break. Rest for a few minutes, maybe go hit some short shots, then come back to the full swing. I don't object to that kind of cycle, if you have enough time.

I also suggest that if you start having a lot of trouble with your swing on the practice tee and can't seem to get it corrected, quit for the day. If you don't, you will just keep trying harder and harder, which means you will swing harder and harder. The tension will build up; you will get worse and worse and soon become totally discouraged.

Some days are better than others. If you are having a bad one, back off and start over tomorrow. A new thought may occur to you, your body will be more rested and you might be amazed at how much more effective your swing is on the new day.

Now that I've told you what *not* to do, what *does* constitute effective practice? The key is *consistency* of practice. Hitting balls for 15 minutes every day, or half an hour every two or three days, will improve you a lot faster than beating them for two or three hours once a week or once every couple of weeks. You will be physically fresher during each session, and the constant repetition will help your swing thoughts stay with you and will ingrain them faster. You may think you are proceeding at a slow pace, but you really are not.

I find that sometimes I get an idea on the practice tee—I'm still learning the game, just as everybody else is—but it might not sink in right away. I have to get away, go home and do something else before something clicks and I can put the idea to work in the next practice session.

You may have had that same kind of experience taking a lesson from your professional. Maybe what he told you to do didn't work at the time. Perhaps you were a little nervous or self-conscious taking the lesson. But when you got away from the range and started thinking about the advice you were given, it made sense. The next time out, it was a lot easier to do. So that's a further advantage to shorter, more frequent workouts.

I believe in acquiring a certain feel and working toward a certain goal, and each day's practice session should be directed toward that. Just to go out and beat balls with no specific purpose in mind is a waste of time. I'd suggest that when you practice, you constantly review the fundamentals of grip, setup, use of the left arm and use of the legs, plus the tempo aids that can help you put them all together into a good swing. If you are having a particular problem, go back over your checklist. If you can, have somebody observe you—your professional, a friend, or even your wife or husband, someone who has seen you play and might be able to spot a trouble area in your setup or swing.

If you are really serious about improving, you might invest in a videotape machine, if you can afford it, or a movie camera and a projector with slow-motion and stop-action capability. A motor-drive camera that takes several frames a second is useful also. I didn't see my own swing on film until I was 18 years old, and when I did I solved a big problem. I had been dipping my head three or four inches on the backswing. People would tell me about it, but I just couldn't hold it still, and it was causing me to be very inconsistent. Finally, a friend took some movies of my swing, and after watching them about 15 times I figured out what I was doing. That was in the days when professionals used to advocate keeping your left heel on the ground throughout the swing. When I did that, the bending of my left leg would cause my whole left side to collapse and dip down. So I just started letting my left heel come off the ground on the backswing, and this let my head stay steady. That helped me turn the corner in my career, and ever since I've taken movies and sequence pictures of my swing two or three times a year.

Nobody ever swings as he thinks he does, so film or videotape accomplishes one important thing—it changes the picture in your mind from what you think you look like to what you actually look like during your swing. Then, when you make changes and improvements, you can picture your swing as it is rather than as something it isn't.

Be sure when you take movies or any pictures of your swing that the camera is square to and centered on your body. If you are taking pictures from behind, or down the target line, be sure the camera is centered on a line halfway between your toes and the ball and is square to that line. Distortions from either of those angles can give you errone-ous information, particularly concerning your posture, aim, alignment and ball position.

Reviewing the fundamental areas is especially important if you are just learning the game. After you learn certain things in a swing, they come almost automatically. That's why it is so important to learn the proper way to do things. If you learn the wrong method, that also becomes automatic, and it is hard to make changes in the golf swing.

While you want to constantly review your fundamentals, it is also important that you only *work on one thing at a time*. If you have some swing changes to make, make them one at a time. And think of only one thing when you make a swing. (That's good advice at any time, especial-ly on the course.) You might have three or four swing thoughts or feels that you want to work on or change, but you won't accomplish anything by thinking of them all at once. The mind can't handle it.

That's the problem with going to your professional for a lesson. If he knows he is only going to see you one time, he may give you four or five suggestions. They may all be valid, but they won't do you any good because you will be thinking of them all at once and won't be able to execute the swing. He would be doing you a great favor by suggesting a series of lessons, each dealing with one particular point. And you would be doing yourself a favor by agreeing to that.

You can concern yourself with more than one thought or change in the areas of grip and setup because those are accomplished before the swing begins. But when you get ready to start that swing, you should have just one key thought in your mind. Work with that one thought for a while, then, the next day or a couple of sessions later, start working with another, and so on. By incorporating your changes slowly, you'll actually

Vary the distance in practice

When you are practicing your short game, whether it be pitching, chipping, sand play or putting, vary your targets to acquire a feel for distance. When you are pitching (left), spot shag bags or other objects at various distances. On the putting green (right), putt to different holes or to tees stuck in the turf. Never hit a shot or a putt to the same target more than twice in a row.

master each one of them much faster.

Practice Session Structure

The actual routine of your practice session should cover all areas of the game. Start out with a short iron—a wedge or 9-iron—and swing slowly for a few shots. I'll expand on that point in a moment. Then go through the bag, hitting full shots, although you don't have to hit every club. If, however, you are making a change or trying to correct a particular problem, you might just select one iron that is easy to hit, say a 5-iron or 7-iron, and work with that club until you get your problem solved.

I never hit a lot of driver shots on the practice tee, because if I do, my tempo starts getting faster and faster and I'm doing more damage than good. I think you too ought to be careful in that regard.

When you practice, always pick a specific target for each shot, and always go through your pre-shot routine. That will make you more

target-oriented on the course and more apt to maintain a consistent routine.

Never neglect the short game, as many players do. In fact, you ought to devote more time to that than you do to the full swing. Hit some chips, some pitches, some trap shots and some putts, varying your target and distance as I described earlier.

Spend some time practicing out of the rough if at all possible. Hit both short shots and full shots from the heavy grass. Not only will this teach you how to hit those shots, but swinging repeatedly through the heavy stuff will improve your acceleration on normal swings.

As you are practicing, whether it be the long game or short, never lose sight of your tempo regardless of how much you are working with the mechanics of your swing. One of the biggest mistakes any of us makes is concentrating so hard on the mechanics that we forget the tempo and timing that puts the swing together and makes it work. So never *ever* leave the practice tee without devoting some time to your tempo. Work with some of the tempo keys I suggested earlier. Don't think about what you have just been working on mechanically. Instead, end your session by simply trying to make some smooth, well-paced swings. You'll find that will make your mechanics better than ever.

And don't forget that golf is a game to be played, not just a game of making swings. Don't overlook the value of playing a few holes occasionally in the evening, maybe hitting two or three balls if the course is not crowded. This gives you the advantage of being able to take your swing out on the course and work with it when you're not faced with an 18-hole round and a $2 nassau riding on it. Once your swing is reasonably sound in terms of fundamentals, on-course practice will do you more good than the same amount of time spent on the practice tee.

Finally, your attitude toward practice is important. I enjoy hitting golf balls. I loved to practice when I was a kid and I still do. You should develop that attitude too. Practice should be something you *want* to do, not something you *have* to do. You should look on it as a chance to get away from the house or the office, get out in the fresh air and have some fun, not to mention improving your golf game at the same time. This attitude will relax you and make your practice sessions that much more effective.

Pre-Round Preparation

It is vital to establish your tempo for the day at the very start of your round. Rather, it is vital to your success to establish the *correct* tempo. You might have spent all week on the practice tee preparing for your Saturday round, but if you don't prepare properly Saturday morning, your efforts will have been wasted.

There are several ways to set the right tempo for your round, and I'll list them here in order of their effectiveness.

The best way to prepare is to hit some balls on the practice range. Start slowly with a short iron and hit a few shots with, say, every other club. Pick your target, go through your routine and work only on your tempo. You are not practicing; you are preparing yourself to play. All you want to do is get loose and acquire a feel for the swing that you will be using that day. I wouldn't hit more than a couple dozen balls or so. If you hit more than that, you are liable to start swinging faster. You also may wear yourself out and tire in the middle of the round. Don't hit many drivers, and finish your warm-up by hitting a few soft wedge shots and some putts. This takes you to the first tee with the feeling of a slower tempo ingrained.

Often, of course, you don't have time to hit balls before you play—or at least you don't make the time. And when I'm not on tour and am just playing friendly rounds at home, I'm just as guilty as anybody of arriving at the first tee two minutes before I'm due to tee off. I've learned a few tricks that help in these cases. If I have a few free moments at home before I drive to the course, I go out in the yard and swing a club, slowly at first, then gradually making a bigger, faster swing. This gets the blood pumping, and I'm always amazed at how loose I am by the time I reach the course. Or you might keep a club in the office and swing it a few times prior to heading for the course from there.

If you don't have time for that program, the third best thing is to take some practice swings before you tee off. Try to allow a couple of minutes, after you do so, to give the blood time to circulate and loosen the muscles.

Finally, if your group is calling your name as you walk to the tee and you have to hit that first shot cold turkey, then *swing the way you feel*. The player who feels stiff on the first tee and swings hard to overcome that stiffness, as most do, is in real trouble. In the first place, he has established a tempo that is far too fast. He has probably hit a bad shot, which upsets him, and he swings harder and faster on the next shot. It all goes downhill from there. Six holes later he might calm down, or maybe give up, and play pretty well from there on in, but he has already ruined his round of golf.

When I find myself in a situation like that on the first tee, I give it what I call my *slow-motion swing*. And I mean it's really slow. I don't care how far it goes; I just want to get the clubface on the ball. And there it goes, boom, down the middle and pretty far, and everybody swears I've been over hitting balls. Of course, I can do that because I have a pretty sound swing. But you can help yourself too with the same approach. If you feel stiff, just swing slowly and easily on that first shot. Your muscles aren't ready for a hard swing. By swinging slowly and easily, you will be in control of your swing. Your timing will be much better and you will develop a lot more clubhead speed than if you flail at the ball. You might be amazed at how well and how far you hit it.

Keep that slow thought in mind on the following shots too. If you are 7-iron distance from the flag, take a 6- or 5-iron. Swing easy. And take a few practice swings while you are waiting for the others to hit. Soon your body will respond and you will be able to get back to normal. In the meantime, you have accomplished a couple of important things—you have avoided ruining your round with a series of missed shots and bad holes, and you have established a tempo that will let you play well for the rest of the day.

CHAPTER TWELVE

TEMPO AND THE MIND

Throughout this book I have tried to make it clear how soundness in the fundamental areas is instrumental in developing the correct tempo for you. In closing, I'd like to make equally clear how important your attitude, your mental approach to golf, is in maintaining that good tempo.

To keep your swing operating at the right pace on the course, you must keep your mind under control. You must have an attitude that lets you maintain your composure.

Fortunately, I've been blessed with a pretty good attitude all my life. The older I get, the more I realize how important that good attitude is and the more I see how the lack of it ruins a lot of potentially good players at all levels. I see it on the professional tour, which maybe is not surprising, because we play golf for a living and it's easy enough to lose your cool with the rent money at stake. But I also see this problem at every other level of golf. I've even told a few people that they should not play the game, because I've noticed that all they do when they get on the golf course is torture themselves. They are so uptight about playing well and there is such a battle within themselves whenever they miss a shot or fail at what they are trying to do, they just don't enjoy the game at all. Honestly, I advise them,to quit playing and have one less problem in life to worry about.

The key to creating the right attitude is to remember *why* you play golf. You play it for fun. You do not play it for an annual income. You make your living doing something else, and no doubt you take that with proper seriousness. But golf gives you the chance to do something different. It gives you the chance to get out in the fresh air and enjoy the beautiful countryside, relaxing, getting exercise. It gives you a chance to play a game, to realize the enjoyment of performing a skill by hitting a good shot once in a while. It tests you mentally. You are playing strategically against the course and internally against yourself. And that challenge may be the biggest reason why golf is the great game that it is.

Even though I play golf for a living, I enjoy it. I guess I'm lucky to be able to earn a living doing something that I enjoy so much. I don't think I could play well enough to make a living if I didn't have fun doing it.

Attitude boils down to a matter of how much pressure you put on yourself. You must remember that you play golf at your own level, and you can enjoy it at any level. It doesn't make any difference how well somebody else plays. Don't relate your game to others. Whether you are a 75 or a 125 shooter, whether you are 8 or 80 years old, whether you are naturally athletic or poorly coordinated, the challenge of golf lies in playing it as well as *you* can.

Recognize your level of ability and don't expect too much out of yourself. Don't put too much pressure on yourself to improve too fast. Don't put too much pressure on yourself to hit a lot of good shots. The less pressure you put on yourself to hit a good shot every time, the more you will enjoy the game . . . and the more good shots you will hit.

Too many players hit one good shot and think every shot after that should be a good one. When that doesn't happen, they fall apart and pretty soon are tied up in knots.

Test yourself by analyzing your rounds of golf. Note where you hit a bad shot in a particular round and see if that didn't start a chain reaction of bad shots. Inability to accept a bad shot, which causes the subsequent rash of bad shots, may be the most common downfall among amateurs. Once you let a bad shot affect your composure, your tempo goes down the drain and disaster follows.

Golf is a game of misses. Never does even the best player hit all his shots the way he wants to. Seldom do you—or I—hit more than a very few shots the way we want to. The secret is in keeping your misses playable, somewhere on the golf course instead of over the adjoining road, and in not being bothered by those misses.

If you hit a bad shot, just tell yourself it is great to be alive, relaxing and walking around on a beautiful golf course. The next shot will be better. This attitude will relax you, will slow down your tempo and will, indeed, make the next shot better.

I'm not saying you should not be competitive on the golf course. Far from it. Competition, both against yourself and others, is part of the fun. There is a great satisfaction in winning. But you'll find that the more you approach the game with a relaxed attitude, the more fun you have, the more competitive you will be. Your tempo will be better, you will hit better shots and have a better chance of winning and shooting lower scores.

You can better keep your mind under control and give yourself a running start toward good tempo if you develop a consistent pre-shot routine, one in which your preparations are the same for every swing.

It doesn't really matter how you make those preparations as long as you follow some common-sense guidelines. Basically, you pick your target and establish your target line from behind the ball. You can assume your grip as you walk to the ball or as you stand beside it, making sure your hands are on the club correctly *before* you line up the clubface. From slightly behind the ball, step in with your right foot, aim the clubface at your target and complete your setup as I've described. Take a waggle or two, moving the club back and forth along the target line with your left hand. While you do this, take a final look or two at the target, then start your swing.

What is important is that you go through this routine the same way every time and in approximately the same amount of time. This gets your body accustomed to a certain way to begin the swing, giving it a preliminary feel that moves you smoothly into the swing without thinking about how to start. This frees your mind to concentrate on the target and the shot you are about to make.

If you work on this in practice, especially that portion of your practice during which you are trying to put your swing together, you will find a pre-shot routine easier to do on the course. And the better you can perform your routine on the course, the better you will be able to overcome tension.

Whenever I see a player I know deviate from his normal routine when he prepares to hit a pressure shot, I know that the tension has got to him. I can also predict pretty accurately that his shot won't be very good. He has allowed the situation to destroy his confidence in his routine and consequently his swing.

One of the best I've seen at keeping his routine constant in the most critical situations is Lee Trevino. He takes the same amount of time and makes the same moves for a shot that will win him a major championship as he does in a practice round.

In either case, Lee spends very little time over the ball, and that's pretty good advice for you, too. The longer you stand over the ball before beginning your swing, the more chances you give your mind to start working and your muscles to get tight. Most of us can't hit it as quickly as Trevino does, but we can develop a smooth pre-shot routine that doesn't waste any time.

Your routine, by the way, should be followed on every shot, including your putts. When Tom Weiskopf had his great season in 1974, I've always felt one of the big reasons was that his putting routine was rhythmic and constant all season long. It hasn't been that good since, which may be why Tom hasn't had a year like that since.

The philosophy that governs your strategic approach to the game also can have a great bearing on your attitude, your ability to maintain your composure and subsequently your tempo. By strategic approach I mean what you are basically trying to do with your shots. And the basic principle golf course strategy is—*don't try anything more than your game is ready to handle.* Don't try to pull off a shot you can't hit at your particular stage of development.

It is important that you are *aware* on the course—aware of what you are capable of doing with your shots, aware of the trajectory or height you hit your various clubs, aware of the possibilities for playing a certain shot different ways within the range of your capabilities.

Playing in the Heritage Classic at Harbour Town Golf Links on Hilton Head Island, S.C., one year, I hooked my second shot on the par-5 15th hole well into some palmetto trees and behind a lake. When I got to the ball, a marshal was standing over it, shaking his head. He could see no way I could make the shot. There was what looked like a wall of jungle in front of me, and while I could swing at the ball, there was no apparent way I could get to the fairway, forward or backward. But as I squatted down and looked over the situation, I saw that if I could keep the ball low for the first 20 feet, I could go under a bush and then get it up through a hole in the trees 30 yards away. I took an 8-iron, moved the ball back in my stance, punched it under the bush, through the trees, over the lake and back onto the fairway. As I walked away, the marshal was still shaking his head in disbelief.

I don't always advocate gambles like that,but using your imagination in that manner can save you strokes. It also can be a lot of fun.

One of the biggest aids to relaxation for most players, including me, is to pick a bigger target area. For example, if you have a natural fade or a natural draw, use that to your advantage. If you are a fader, aim down the left side and let the ball work across the fairway. That gives you the whole fairway, a bigger target, to work with. If you aim right up the middle, you really are giving yourself only half the fairway as a target.

The same approach holds true in hitting to the green. I don't fire right at the pin. This causes me to try to steer the ball, to guide it, which disrupts my tempo and inhibits the freedom of my swing. Instead, I aim at a bigger area. I don't even aim at the cup on long putts, choosing instead a larger area in which to try to stop the ball.

This attitude allows me to take a much more relaxed swing—or stroke—at the ball. Because I don't put so much pressure on myself to hit the ball into a specific, tiny area, chances are I will hit my shots much straighter and more consistently. By taking pressure off myself, I improve my tempo, which improves my shotmaking. The same approach will work for you.

The bigger target areas also tip the percentages in our favor. As I indicated earlier, golf is not a game of the one occasional great shot. It is a game of consistency more than pinpoint precision. Instead of trying to hit every shot six inches from the flag, be concerned with hitting more fairways and getting on more greens in regulation figures. You will instinctively be more relaxed, your tempo will be better, your scores will get consistently better and you will enjoy the game a lot more.

If that happens for you, perhaps in some part because of reading this book, then writing it will have been worthwhile for me.